EMPLOYEE DRIVEN QUALITY

**Releasing the Creative Spirit
of Your Organization
Through Suggestion Systems**

EMPLOYEE DRIVEN QUALITY

Releasing the Creative Spirit of Your Organization Through Suggestion Systems

Robin E. McDermott
Raymond J. Mikulak
Michael R. Beauregard

QR QUALITY RESOURCES
A Division of The Kraus Organization Limited
One Water Street, White Plains, New York 10601

Most Quality Resources books are available at discount rates when purchased in bulk. For more information contact:

Special Sales Department
Quality Resources
A Division of The Kraus Organization Limited
One Water Street
White Plains, New York 10601
800-247-8519   914-761-9600

Printed in the United States of America

97 96 95 94 93   10 9 8 7 6 5 4 3 2 1

Quality Resources
A Division of The Kraus Organization Limited
One Water Street
White Plains, New York 10601

∞

The paper used in this publication meets the minimum requirements of American National Standard for Information Sciences—Permanence of Paper for Printed Library Materials, ANSI Z39.48-1984.

ISBN 0-527-91670-6

Library of Congress Cataloging-in-Publication Data
McDermott, Robin E.
    Employee-driven quality : releasing the creative spirit of your
organization through suggestion systems / Robin E. McDermott,
Raymond J. Mikulak, Michael R. Beauregard.
        p.   cm.
    Includes bibliographical references and index.
    ISBN 0-527-91670-6
    1. Suggestion systems.   2. Total quality management.
3. Efficiency, Industrial.   I. Mikulak, Raymond J.   II. Beauregard,
Michael R.   III. Title.
HF5549.5.S8M35   1993
658.5'62—dc20   93-11078
                                                          CIP

Contents

Preface

Total quality has become the operating standard for businesses. Employee involvement and empowerment are becoming the primary means to achieve total quality. Organizations are waking up to the fact that there is tremendous knowledge, strength, and ability within their own ranks. Suddenly, they are enamored by anything that will tap this once ignored resource.

A formal suggestion system seems like a logical fit to a total quality environment. It provides a way for employees to give their ideas for improvement, and the formality of the system assures their suggestions are acted on. Yet companies fall into the trap of building a suggestion system based on those of the past. They design a traditional suggestion system with only the best intentions, and then wonder why it isn't working. It is clear why such systems don't work when you consider these key components to a traditional suggestion system:

- Traditional suggestion systems are fueled by financial incentives for employees to participate, usually in the form of a percentage of the savings realized because of the suggestion. This encourages employees to keep ideas to themselves so they don't have to share the reward money with anyone else. This also discourages managers from approving ideas if large payouts are involved.

- The employee's involvement in the suggestion ends when the idea is submitted. Someone else or a committee is responsible for implementing the suggestion. These others have no vested interest in the idea; they have their own work to do.

Until recently, few other models were available. If you wanted to see examples of suggestion systems that are aligned with the total quality philosophy, you had to look to Japan. Today there are working suggestion systems in the United States that do foster teamwork, that do empower employees to make and act on their ideas, and that are working better than the traditional models. They exist in all sized companies and in both the manufacturing and service sectors.

This book is a "how-to" guide that will help total quality organizations establish suggestion systems that support their existing employee-involvement efforts. To help make the shift from the paradigm of the traditional suggestion system, we are calling this new approach to suggestion systems an Employee-Driven Idea System, or EDIS.

From the name, it's clear that we're talking about something different. In a well-developed EDIS, employees are truly the drivers of their ideas; from inception to implementation, they make their ideas a reality.

An EDIS is one element of a total quality process. *Employee-Driven Quality* will help you integrate your EDIS with the other elements of your total quality process. Chapter by chapter, you'll learn how and why an EDIS works. You'll also learn that an EDIS is just a step in the path to true employee empowerment, to true employee-driven quality.

Chapter 1—The Role of Employee-Driven Idea Systems in Total Quality Management. In this first chapter we review the key elements of Total Quality Management—Creating the Environment, the Continuous Improvement Toolbox, and Employee Empowerment. We'll show where the EDIS fits in the overall total quality strategy.

Chapter 2—What's Wrong With Traditional Suggestion Systems? In this chapter you'll learn why traditional suggestion systems don't work in today's world of high employee involvement and teamwork.

Chapter 3—What Makes an Employee-Driven Idea System Work? Here we discuss how an EDIS differs from a traditional suggestion system and why it logically fits in a total quality environment.

Chapter 4—Recognition or Rewards? This chapter takes the mystery out of "motivating employees" by discussing the pros and cons of these two age-old and controversial topics of business.

Chapter 5—Starting Up an Employee-Driven Idea System. This chapter presents a step-by-step process covering the nuts and bolts of an EDIS.

Chapter 6—Roles and Responsibilities in an Employee-Driven Idea System. This chapter discusses the role each person and group in the organization plays in an EDIS to ensure companywide involvement and to support the evolution of Employee Empowerment.

Chapter 7—Using Continuous Improvement Tools to Generate Ideas. In this chapter we demonstrate how to integrate the continuous improvement process and tools into the EDIS to reinforce existing training and improve the quality of ideas and their implementation.

Chapter 8—Success Stories: Stealing Shamelessly. Here you'll learn about eight companies that have an EDIS in place. We'll review how they got started, where they're at today, and their plans for the future.

Chapter 9—Epilogue: What's Next? This last chapter answers questions such as, Will we always need an EDIS? Or will it eventually evolve into an informal system? Where can an EDIS lead to?

You'll find plenty of examples and ideas throughout this book. We encourage you to "steal shamelessly," and challenge you to improve on everything we've presented to create your own employee-driven quality!

Acknowledgments

This book is a living example of teamwork and involvement throughout the development and publication process. This teamwork brought together a series of customers and suppliers without whom the process would not exist.

Our Suppliers

These are the people who provided grist for the mill, the raw materials, and the polish to help put our words into book form. We are indebted to Judy Stadler of Sheldahl Company, whose Implemented Suggestion System (ISS) sounded like an unorthodox scheme when we first heard about it in 1987. Today the Sheldahl ISS is six years old and going strong; it is a "model" EDIS in the United States—proving that we *needed* a radical change from traditional suggestion systems. Honda of America Manufacturing, Toyota Motor Manufacturing U.S.A., Turbotec Products, AT&T Universal Card Services, Rockwell Space Operations Company, Critikon, and a truck component manufacturer in Connecticut lent substance and form to the book by allowing us to tell stories about their suggestion systems. Eric Harriott helped us communicate our message visually with his graphics. Chiaki Umeno of Otalite Ltd. in Fukuoka, Japan, provided us with an introduction to Toyota Motor Manufacturing.

Our Customers

The people at Quality Resources, the publisher of this book, are everything you'd want in a customer. They made their needs clear by establishing tough quality standards and setting rigorous deadlines. Yet they were always understanding when our material (the manuscript) was on back order to them. Their skill and experience turned our raw materials into a product we can all be proud of.

Our goal for this book is to delight you, our ultimate customer, by showing you how to tap into the creativity, knowledge, and skills of your work force. We are grateful to everyone in our extended customer-supplier process who has helped us achieve our objective.

Robin E. McDermott, C.Q.E.
Raymond J. Mikulak, P.E., C.Q.E.
Michael R. Beauregard, P.E., C.Q.E.

Chapter 1

The Role of Employee-Driven Idea Systems in Total Quality Management

Your Organization's Most Valuable Resource—People

What is an organization's most valuable resource? It's not the balance sheet, the facilities, or capital equipment; it's not even the technology. It's the people. Only people can work the systems and the equipment, apply the technology, and improve the balance sheet.

However, to paraphrase W. Edwards Deming, from his description of the "deadly diseases" in his video *Management's Five Deadly Diseases*[1], the United States is perhaps the country with the most underdeveloped natural resources—people—in the industrialized world. Our people, as employees, says Deming, are "underused, abused, and misused." They are trying as hard as they can to do the best

---

[1] *Management's Five Deadly Diseases: A Conversation with W. Edwards Deming* (Chicago: Encyclopedia Britannica Education Corporation, 1984).

1

they can, but as they try to help their organizations excel, they are hampered with:

- a foggy sense of direction;
- fear of reprisal;
- poor problem-solving tools;
- an unclear sense of the limits of their authority.

Total Quality—Unlocking the Shackles

How can we remove the shackles we have used to bind employees? This question may sound like a severe condemnation of our management practices, but the employees' lack of direction, workplace fears, poorly developed skills, and unclear boundaries of freedom (or authority to act) are indeed shackles. If we can remedy these basic systemic flaws, we can release the creative spirit and skills of our employees, our organization's most valuable resource.

Total Quality (TQ) holds the key to unlocking the shackles holding employees back. Only a TQ approach can address the workplace cultural issues that focus on development, not control, of employees. A TQ process strives to create an organizational culture that fosters continuous improvements:

- in everything
  - by *everyone*
    - *all of the time!*

Three Key Elements of Total Quality

The three key elements to TQ are (see Figure 1.1):

1. Creating the Environment
2. The Continuous Improvement (CI) Toolbox
3. Employee Empowerment

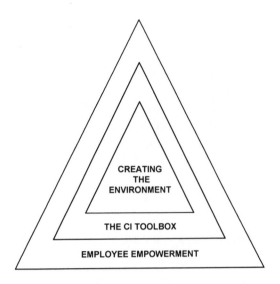

FIGURE 1.1.   The Three Key Elements of TQM

Creating the Environment

The first element, Creating the Environment, is at the core of TQ. It's the job of top management. Only top management can address workplace cultural issues. Fundamental to this is the development of (a) a Vision Statement, (b) Guiding Principles, and (c) a Total Quality Management (TQM) Roadmap (or strategy) to work toward the vision.

The Vision Statement acts as a compass for the organization; it gives the organization a macro-sense of direction; it creates alignment. The Guiding Principles express an organization's overriding values and beliefs; they summarize the way we will *always* conduct ourselves. The TQM Roadmap is an integrated business improvement strategy giving us a series of additive and sequential milestones that are tangible and measurable so we can track our progress toward the vision.

Only management can create an environment in which employees feel comfortable suggesting ideas and improvements that break with the safe haven of the past. After all, what is an improvement?

Improvement means change; it means change for the better, but change nonetheless. And change can be threatening. Change creates stress for both the initiator of the improvement and for the organization faced with a new way of doing business.

Traditionally, employees have been taught that their ideas for improvement aren't valued. They have not been told their ideas are not wanted; suggestion systems have been around for years with the expressed intent of soliciting employees' ideas. But employees know their ideas aren't valued when:

- their supervisors procrastinate in responding to their ideas;
- their supervisors write the idea on a scrap of paper and misplace it;
- they are told their ideas will cost too much to put into practice; and
- they are told, "It's been thought of before," or, "We tried that eight years ago and it didn't work then so it probably won't work now."

Why the traditional hesitancy? Historically, employee ideas and suggestions have been evaluated by management. After all, management has a broader view of the organization. Only it knows the direction and the resources available to the organization. Employees usually aren't privy to the direction or resources of the company, so their ideas for improvement are frequently in conflict with the organization's direction, require resources that aren't available, or are presented in a format not easily understood by management.

In addition, in most organizations employees have never been provided information or training on how to generate ideas or how to develop them. Employees know only their own job. It's unfortunate to think that they know their job and are better at it than anyone else and yet they can't get their ideas for improvement in their area implemented.

How can we tap the creative thoughts and talents of all employees? How can we make it "safe" for employees to go public with ideas they know can improve their jobs, their products and services, and their company? It starts with the culture of the organization, with the daily work environment.

Alignment Through Vision

Most organizations *are* aligned, and employees know their role. The unspoken "aligning vision" is often management's version of "My way or the highway." It may not be the publicly spoken "vision," but it's the one that's implicitly understood. Actions always speak louder than words; if management's actions back up a "my way" approach, that's all that matters to the rest of the organization. Employees will do precisely what they need to do to satisfy "the boss." They may be told that more is expected of them, but they know in reality that they had better:

- do what they're told to do
- not make waves
- realize it's not their job to change things
- understand it's not their job to think of improvements
- know that their job is just to do . . .

This type of message is always received loud and clear. It may not be the message intended by management, but if management reinforces it with its actions, it's the only message the rest of the organization will receive.

How can management turn things around? How can management communicate and reinforce a positive Vision with positive action? It must first start with an empowering Vision that gives everyone the same bird's-eye view of the company's purpose and direction. Then it must reinforce that vision with a set of Guiding Principles that define the fundamental values and beliefs that all in the organization must live by. Organizational alignment is derived from the overriding direction of the Vision and the basic ethical standards clarified by the Guiding Principles.

Three Examples of Vision Statements and Guiding Principles

Let's look at the Vision statements of three organizations. The Visions, with their corresponding Guiding Principles (that clarify and

TABLE 1.1. Vision and Guiding Principles—Imo Airfoil Division

 **Airfoil Division**
Imo Industries Inc.

OUR VISION

We will become unbeatable in providing
Manufactured Turbomachinery Products and Services with
uncompromised quality, rapid turnaround
and exceptional value

OUR GUIDING PRINCIPLES

❑ Anything short of total customer satisfaction is unacceptable.

❑ Welcome innovation and new ideas.

❑ Treat our customers, suppliers and employees fairly, honestly and as partners.

❑ Create an environment that encourages team work and open communication.

❑ Practice continuous improvement as a way of life.

❑ Use our accumulated experience to take calculated risks every day.

❑ Be a leader in ensuring a safe and environmentally sound work place.

❑ Provide resources for training and encourage self improvement.

❑ Conduct our business in an ethical manner at all times.

Reprinted with permission.

communicate the fundamental organizationwide values and beliefs) helped align the organizational efforts of Imo Airfoil Division, PMP Corporation, and Rushford Center, Inc.

We have chosen these three examples because they represent three significantly different types of organizations, but their Vision Statements and Guiding Principles are similar in both power and simplicity.

- Imo Airfoil Division (Table 1.1) is a manufacturing division of Imo Industries, a Fortune 500 company.
- PMP Corporation (Table 1.2) is a small, privately owned and operated remanufacturing (rebuilding) operation.
- Rushford Center (Table 1.3) is a private, not-for-profit organization that provides substance-abuse services.

How can three such dissimilar organizations have so much in common when it comes to Vision Statements and Guiding Principles? It's because their management sought to align their organizational efforts by focusing on the essence of their business—their positive and inspiring Vision of the future—and back it up with a straightforward summary of the basic values all must live by, the Guiding Principles. These Vision Statements speak to their respective ''Vision communities,'' composed of:

- their customers
- their suppliers
- their employees

In each case the Vision Statement explains:

- specifically what the organization does;
- its market;
- its specific differentiating strategic advantages.

The Vision explains in a positive and inspiring way where the organization is going; it gets the whole organization to stretch toward

TABLE 1.2.   Mission (Vision) and Guiding Principles—PMP Corporation

 # PMP CORPORATION

OUR MISSION

PMP is the leading remanufacturer of service station fuel dispensing equipment with the goal of providing products that perform better and last longer than new. Our mission is to continually improve our products and services and to seek out new product opportunities.

OUR GUIDING PRINCIPLES

☐   We will serve our internal and external customers in a manner that will result in recommendations to others. This will be accomplished by a total commitment to quality and continuous improvement in every aspect of our business.

☐   Integrity is never compromised. Our business will be conducted in a manner that is socially and environmentally responsible.

☐   Our people are our most valuable resource. Development through training and education will be an ongoing process.

☐   Customers, suppliers, and fellow employees are partners. We must do error-free work as a responsible link in the chain.

☐   We will foster an atmosphere which encourages mutual respect, listening, an open exchange of ideas, creativity and teamwork.

☐   Creating new products and services to meet our customers' needs will provide future employment opportunities for our people.

☐   Profits are necessary to generate funds for the growth of PMP, to share with our fellow employees, and finally to provide a fair return on investment to our stockholders.

Reprinted with permission.

TABLE 1.3.   Vision and Guiding Principles—Rushford Center

RUSHFORD CENTER
Vision

To make a significant contribution
to reducing substance abuse in Connecticut
by helping individuals, families, and community
create a positive pathway to the future.

Guiding Principles

1. We empower people to improve the quality of life by actively creating conditions for positive action and change.
2. We serve people regardless of their ability to pay.
3. We are committed to our clients for as long as it takes.
4. Recovery is a process and an outcome.
5. We strive to continuously improve everything we do, every day.
6. We are committed to innovation as a way of life at Rushford Center.
7. Honesty is the hallmark of all our relationships.
8. We model for our clients self-respect, self-improvement, respect for others, and personal responsibility through the way we work together as colleagues.
9. Each of us strives for excellence through training and professional development.
10. We prove the value of our services.

Reprinted with permission.

the future. At Imo Airfoil they're redefining the meaning of "rapid turnaround" in the manufactured turbomachinery market. PMP is remanufacturing products "that perform better and last longer than new." And the Rushford Center is working to establish a new paradigm in substance-abuse treatment and prevention by creating "a positive pathway to the future."

These Vision Statements are concise, clear, and comprehensive; they align their organizations. Their vision communities understand the message they deliver.

The Guiding Principles of each organization are elegant in their simplicity. These organizations chose not to write flowery, lengthy prose but instead to provide a clear, understandable recap of values for all to live by.

The management team of The Kraus Organization Limited has identified six characteristics of Guiding Principles. They must:

1. Apply companywide
2. Be relevant to company activities
3. Be positive
4. Be clear and understandable
5. Be *actionable*
6. Be *absolute*

The last two, *actionable* and *absolute* are strong yet necessary statements. They give the Guiding Principles the proper emphasis.

The TQM Roadmap

The Vision acts as the compass pointing the way to the future. The Guiding Principles give us a foundation to judge the appropriateness of our actions. But we need a clear pathway to the promise, a strategy to focus and prioritize our effort toward the Vision. We call that strategy the TQM Roadmap.

The roadmap gives us a way to track our progress toward the Vision with tangible and measurable milestones along the way. We can build the roadmap by breaking the business down into its interdependent functional areas, or roads. Then we identify where we are now and where we need to go on each road in order to reach our goal, the Vision. With the two ends of the road identified, we can develop checkpoints, additive in nature, that will move us from the present to the planned future. The roadmap is the compilation of these interrelated roads.

In a TQ process, the roadmap encompasses every aspect of the business. It becomes the summary of the overall strategic plan for improving business processes. One broad, comprehensive model for a TQM Roadmap is contained in the Malcolm Baldrige National Quality Award criteria (MBNQA, or the "Baldrige").[2] Many think of the Baldrige only as an award, but the Baldrige criteria actually provide an effective model for developing a business improvement strategy. The seven main categories of the Baldrige criteria give us a solid format for running a business; they serve as the framework for laying out our TQM Roadmap.

The seven categories comprising the Baldrige are:

1. Leadership
2. Information and Analysis
3. Strategic Quality Planning
4. Human Resources Development and Management
5. Management of Process Quality
6. Quality and Operational Results
7. Customer Focus and Satisfaction

As shown in Figure 1.2, this model can be organized with leadership (category 1) as the driver of the infrastructure (categories 2 through 5) toward the goal of customer satisfaction (category 7) with measures of progress (category 6) along the way. Table 1.4 is Imo Airfoil's TQM Roadmap (Roadmap to Excellence) based on the Baldrige model. Note column 4.2—Recognition; step 6 is "Develop an Employee-Driven Idea System."

The Continuous Improvement Toolbox

The Continuous Improvement (CI) Toolbox is the second key element of Total Quality. The CI *toolbox* is simply a way of looking at the

---

[2] *1993 Award Criteria, Malcolm Baldrige National Quality Award* (Gaithersburg, MD: National Institute of Standards and Technology, 1993).

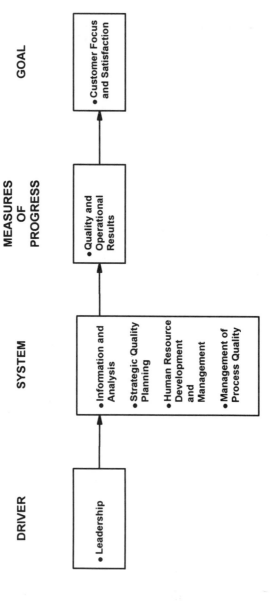

FIGURE 1.2. The MBNQA Criteria as a Framework for the TQM Roadmap

TABLE 1.4. TQM Roadmap—Imo Airfoil Division—A Roadmap to Excellence

STEP	1.0 LEADERSHIP	2.0 INFO & ANALYSIS	3.0 STRATEGIC PLANNING	4.1 TRAINING	4.2 RECOGNITION	5.0 MGT. OF PROCESS QUAL.	6.0 OPERATIONAL RESULTS	7.0 CUSTOMER SATISFACTION
11		Integrated on-line data base		Full potential of the workforce is realized		Become ISO-9000 certifiable		Customers always repeat & sell us to others
10	TQM Council taking a lead in Professional Associations	Review the whole I&A process every 3 years		Employees participate in defining future training needs	Employee satisfaction is surveyed & trending up	Train all employees in ISO-9000 system	Achieve one week lead time for emergency deliveries	Level of customer compliments up & complaints down
9	Environmental leadership & ethical business practices	Establish a benchmarking process	Use it, review it, revise it	Create a training resource team	Employees trained & involved in hiring peers	Audit the system, make repairs, & audit again	Critical financial trends improving	Capture ratio is up
8	Establish a process for rolling out new procedures	Establish a storage & data retrieval network	Translate plans into action	Provide resources for training & encourage self-improvement	Shop personnel involved in visits by customers to our location	Supplier audits are established	Monitor product returns, use to make corrections	One joint paper with a customer per year
7	Council members lead by example with project participation	Process for documentation & control of the data system	Determine what resources are required to make the plan	Conduct formal training needs assessment	Expand boundaries of freedom	Develop a plan to use SPC to control processes	Monitor on-time shipments, continuously improve	Customer satisfaction relative to competition improving
6	Hold regular Div. & dept. communication forums with all	Determine how the data is to be used for continuous improvement	Flowchart the strategic planning process	New employee orientation	Develop an employee-driven idea system	COQ is tracked & used for root cause determination	Establish supplier quality & delivery performance measures	Start customer round tables
5	Systematically encourage innovation & new ideas	Determine how to publicize & transmit the data	Link plans to what's important to the customer	Cross training is part of everyone's job responsibility	Improve recognition process for service awards	Write the IMO Airfoil process manual	Track manufacturing cycle time	On-site survey of customers every year
4	Develop & use a CI project mgt. process	Train people on what data we have & how we use it	Determine who our competition is & why we lose jobs to them	Establish a training curriculum & budget	Safety performance recognized	Establish a process control plan	Establish scrap & rework measures	Develop customer survey process
3	Communicate the Vision, Guiding Principles, & Roadmap	Ensure the data collection methods & info are valid	Analyze the "Contura" product market	Train all employees in TQM principles	Develop a process for recognizing individuals & teams	Upgrade the quality manual	Implement set-up time reductions & monitor	Phone follow-up on all commercial customer orders
2	Develop the Vision, Guiding Principles & Roadmap	Determine who will collect what data & when	Analyze the market	Train the TQM Trainers	TQM Council benchmarks recognition approaches	Internal TQM surveys are conducted	Engineering process analyzed, monitored, & improved	Develop complaint & compliment tracking systems
1	TQM Council established	Identify what data is currently collected	Formalize a short term strategic plan	Tuition reimbursement available to all employees	"Instantaneous" recognition	Train quality personnel in ISO-9000 requirements	Order entry process analyzed, monitored, & improved	Formalize partnership agreement with sister divisions

Reprinted with permission.

13

many continuous improvement tools at our disposal and recognizing they are *not* isolated tools (see Table 1.5). The tools of CI work best when we use them in an integrated way.

The CI team problem-solving process is the basic starting point; it's the foundation for applying all CI tools. Team problem-solving involves a commonsense, six-step approach for making improvements. We call this a "team process," but it works equally well for

---

TABLE 1.5.   Basic Tools in the CI Toolbox

Process Definition Tools

- Flowcharts
- Workflow diagrams

Data Collection & Display Tools

- Checklists
- Tally sheets
- Bar charts
- Pie charts
- Scatter diagrams
- Histograms
- Concentration diagrams
- Trend charts
- Surveys

Team Process Problem-Solving Tools

- Roles & ground rules
- Meeting planners & meeting minutes
- Brainstorming
- Cause & effect diagrams
- Pareto diagrams
- Voting & ranking
- PERT charts
- Activity plans
- Project team reports

---

individual problem-solving activities or projects as well. The six steps are:[3]

Step 1 Set the Team
Step 2 Clarify the Objective
Step 3 Find the Major Causes (the Root Causes)
Step 4 Identify the Most Likely Solution
Step 5 Develop and Implement the Action Plan
Step 6 Evaluate and Adjust

These six steps are further detailed in Figure 1.3.

The six-step problem-solving process is really a problem-finding, problem-solving process. We should spend 75 percent of our time in steps 1 through 3 to ensure we understand the process and find the root cause. Once we have found the root cause, solving the problem (steps 4–5) is usually straightforward. Too often, in the rush to "just do it" we skip steps 1–3 and end up with a band-aid fix to a symptom, not a lasting solution to the root cause.

While the CI process is the basic starting point, intermediate and advanced tools are available to supplement and complement the team process (see Table 1.6). However, regardless of whether we're applying statistical tools, inventory management and cycle-time reduction tools, procedural-improvement tools or performance-measurement tools, they all work better with the solid foundation of teamwork and the team process in place. Because most improvements will cross internal customer-supplier lines, it's only natural that teamwork be the foundation of any improvement effort.

Employee Empowerment

The third key element of Total Quality is Employee Empowerment. Empowerment is evolutionary; it expands slowly over time. Empow-

---

[3]Source: Mikulak, Raymond J., Robin E. McDermott, and Michael R. Beauregard, *First Class Service: The Training System for Continuous Quality Improvement* (White Plains, NY: Quality Resources, 1991).

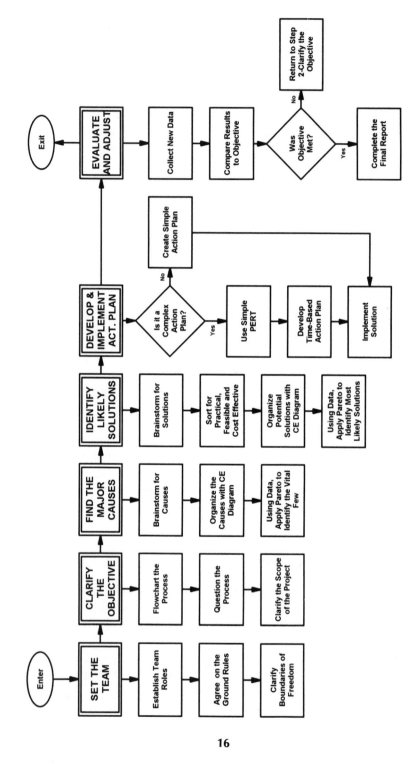

FIGURE 1.3. The Continuous Improvement Team Problem-Solving Process

16

TABLE 1.6. TQ Tools

Basic Tools	**CI Process**-Continuous improvement process. The framework for all of the basic problem-finding, problem-solving, and team tools *Kaizen*-a Japanese term that, loosely translated, means constant continuous improvement
Intermediate Tools	**SPC**-statistical process control **JIT**-just in time **FMEA**-failure mode and effect analysis **TPM**-total productive maintenance **ISO-9000**-an international standard defining the minimum components of a quality management system **MBNQA**-the Malcolm Baldrige National Quality Award
Advanced Tools	**DOE**-design of experiments **QFD**-quality function deployment **Benchmarking**-searching for best practices

erment can't exist for long without the first two elements. Empowered employees need the direction an aligning vision provides plus the structure and tools the CI Process and CI Toolbox contain.

The "Brainline"

There's more to empowerment, however. We can't just let people know where we're going, give them the tools and tell them, "Now you're empowered." We have to recognize that for years we've controlled organizations with what can be called a brainline (see Figure 1.4). Most organizations have a brainline.[4] It's that line, often invisible to top management, that lies somewhere between the top level and the "worker level," and that differentiates "those who think"

---

[4]Brainline concept from seminar given by James F. Leonard, October 30, 1989.

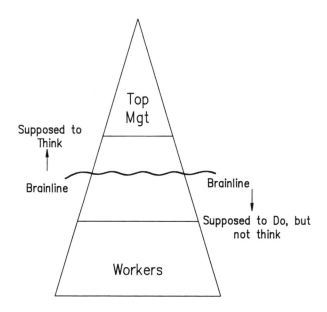

FIGURE 1.4.   The Organizational Brainline

from "those who do"—and aren't expected to think. If you're above the brainline, it's part of your job to think, to come up with new ideas and create new products, processes, and services. But if you're below the brainline, your job is to know all of the policies, procedures, and methods and carry them out flawlessly everyday. You are expected to check your brain at the door because thinking is only for those "above" you.

As we stated before, the existence of a brainline is often a surprise to the top-management team. However, almost every other employee in an organization knows about it and knows which side of the brainline he or she is on. The brainline has nothing to do with an employee's education level. We once worked with an environmental engineering firm in which almost every employee possessed an advanced degree yet all but the four owners claimed they were *below* the brainline. Similarly, in most hospitals highly educated nurses tell us they, too, are below the brainline. What a waste of talent, creativity, and brain power! What a source of frustration to the employee and management team alike. The brainline doesn't benefit anyone.

To erase the brainline, the management team must:

1. *Acknowledge that it exists.* This is tougher than it seems. No one wants to admit they are suppressing brain power. But if you've ever thought to yourself, "I can do it better myself," or if you've told someone they are doing something wrong when there is no "right way," but they aren't doing it *your* preferred way, then you are guilty of establishing a brainline.
2. *Publicly communicate that, now that the brainline has been "discovered," it will be driven out of the organization.* This is a tough, but necessary, step for management. The management team will be more comfortable avoiding a public admission of a brainline in the organization. It's akin to an admission of guilt! However, it's a necessary step to build a TQ environment in which an EDIS can thrive.

TQ is based on continuous improvement founded in teamwork. Continuous improvement is an attitude all must have; teamwork requires mutual trust and respect. Acknowledgment of a brainline by the management team paves the way for a strong foundation of trust and respect. It moves management beyond the denial stage and readies the organization for interdisciplinary teamwork and trust.

How should the management team "announce" its discovery of a brainline? It requires face-to-face group meetings. A word of caution here: be sincere, be honest, be humble, but don't be long-winded or philosophical; keep the meetings short, focused, and tied to the future, and repeat the theme frequently.

1. *Share the Vision with the entire organization to give employees a common, shared sense of direction.* The Vision gives everyone direction and clarifies "which way the winning is" for the organization. Going public with the Vision removes the veil of secrecy surrounding the organization's future direction. We all want to be part of a winning team. Unfortunately, most organizations don't give employees a clue to which direction to take to win.
2. *Communicate the Guiding Principles.* The management team may initially feel the guiding principles are so simple, so obvious, and

so understandable that they speak for themselves. We have never found this to be so. Employees will understand them; the Guiding Principles will sound "good," but they won't necessarily be accepted. Employees will say things such as:

- "Sure, this is the way I would like it to be, but it won't happen here."
- "Are we supposed to do these all of the time? I know we should, but we haven't before."

The Guiding Principles must be embraced by the management team. As Tom McGee, president of PMP Corporation, has said, "Once you go public with your Guiding Principles, you must live them all of the time. Employees will test you. Be sure you really mean them before you unveil them."

3. *Provide people with the tools (the CI Toolbox) they need to build a winning team.*
4. *And finally, establish boundaries of freedom.*

Boundaries of Freedom

What are boundaries of freedom? At first, the thought of boundaries sounds counter to the concept of empowerment, doesn't it?

Establishing boundaries does limit freedom; boundaries denote a line beyond which we cannot cross. Every job has boundary lines or parts of the job that are beyond an employee's limits to change. Even company owners or CEOs have lines they can't cross, such as federal or state regulations. But with clear and consistently communicated boundaries, employees are truly empowered. The boundaries of freedom show employees where they can't go, but most importantly, also clarify in which areas they are free to act, to change things and to make improvements without additional permission or fear of reprisal (see Figure 1.5).

People want freedom. However, if they don't know the degree to which they do or do not have freedom, they'll be paralyzed, afraid to act. Their perceived boundaries of freedom will be limited to an outline painted around the soles of their shoes. An EDIS requires clear and sensible boundaries. These boundaries, coupled with the basic tools of continuous improvement, will give employees the free-

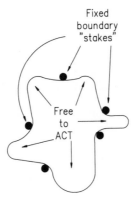

FIGURE 1.5.   Boundaries of Freedom

dom to create and implement new ideas that will help improve the whole organization.

How do we set boundaries of freedom? At first, boundaries need to be "in close"—not quite right around the soles of the shoes, but maybe in a "two-foot circle" around the shoes. This is because clearly and consistently communicated boundaries of freedom help:

- focus people on their job functions.

- empower them to make improvements that deal with their immediate and extended process (see Figure 1.6), involving transactions with

  —their internal supplier;

  —their own process;

  —and their internal customer.

- reinforce the organizational discipline of using the CI Process on individual activities as well as on team projects.

Over time, as trust begins to build, the boundaries of freedom can be expanded. When they are, they again need to be clearly communicated and consistently applied. How does trust build? It's based on past actions. Trust is something that develops between two parties. If both parties do what they say they'll do, the basis for trust is established. In this case, we're referring particularly to trust between the management team and employees.

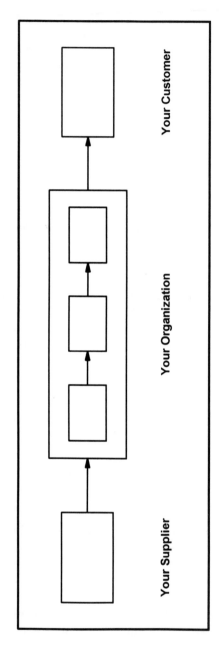

FIGURE 1.6. The Extended Process

What could cause a breakdown of trust? From the management team's perspective: employees have not performed as directed or expected and therefore cannot be trusted to perform "properly" in the future; they need closer supervision, more rules, less options. From the employee's standpoint: management has not followed through on promises or pronouncements. Or individuals may feel that they have done their job properly, taken resourceful initiatives, and yet have had the "rug pulled out from beneath them" because they overstepped their bounds.

In either case, the breakdown of trust is a system or process problem or, as Dr. Deming puts it, a management problem. If employees do not perform as directed or expected by management, it's probable:

- their assignment was not clearly explained.
- their level of training was inadequate.
- the limits (boundaries) of their freedom to take action were not clear.
- the purpose of their assignment was not clear.

If employees don't trust their managers, it's probable:

- supervisors and managers seem to be changing the rules, even if they haven't.
- management may not be living up to the Guiding Principles.
- employees' fear of reprisal is preventing them from taking action, initiating action, or reporting situations needing action.

A TQ environment builds two-way trust by clarifying direction (Vision) and values (Guiding Principles). Clear and consistently communicated boundaries of freedom play a major role in creating a TQ environment.

Establishing boundaries of freedom is crucial to begin the (slow) evolution of Employee Empowerment. Boundaries of freedom validate the link between the first key element of Total Quality—Creating the Environment—and the third, Employee Empowerment. Without boundaries of freedom, even the most aligned organization with the most complete toolbox is like a head without a functioning body. An EDIS cannot thrive in this environment.

Nine Guideposts for Structuring the Boundaries of Freedom

As previously discussed, everyone in every job has boundaries of freedom. The leader of a country or the general of an army have boundaries of freedom. Within any organization, boundaries of freedom will be different for different functional areas and different people, but all boundaries of freedom should be structured around nine central guideposts:

1. Monetary limits
2. Time constraints
3. Schedules and deadlines
4. Access to information
5. Value-adding measures (return on investment; importance; priority)
6. Use of a common problem-solving methodology (the CI Process)
7. Compliance with laws, regulations, and policies
8. Adherence to the Guiding Principles
9. Alignment with the organization's Vision

This set of nine guideposts should be used to establish the boundaries of freedom for any project or activity within an organization. The first five (money, time, schedule, information access, and value-adding determinations) are ''moveable'' guideposts; their placement depends upon:

- the scope of the project;
- the experience of the project participants;
- the level of mutual trust between the project participants and the individual(s) setting the boundaries of freedom.

Mutual trust is, again, a function of past experience; if both parties did what they said they would do in the past, the level of trust (and correspondingly, the boundaries of freedom) is expanded. If, however, the trust was violated, the boundaries of freedom must be reined in until a higher level of mutual trust is earned.

The last four guideposts are not moveable; they're the stationary stakes that anchor the boundary lines. Everyone working on an activity or a project must work with the boundaries of freedom of a common (proven) problem-solving process in compliance with all applicable laws, regulations, and organizational policies, consistent with the Guiding Principles and aligned with the organizational direction defined by the Vision.

Employee Empowerment Is Evolutionary

Employee Empowerment is evolutionary in terms of both boundaries of freedom and structure. From a boundaries-of-freedom standpoint, the five moveable guideposts of boundaries (money, time, schedule, information access, value-adding measure) will, over time, evolve and expand. The organizational structure will also evolve and move through phases of involvement and participation to empowerment over time.

Four Steps Along the Path to Empowerment

In a TQ environment, the organization's structure can evolve through four major steps:

1. CI project teams
2. Employee-Driven Idea Systems
3. Work cells
4. Self-managed work teams

The four steps are interrelated. They reinforce one another if adopted in the sequence suggested. However, different sequences have worked for some organizations.

CI Project Teams

By focused CI project teams, we mean small groups of employees working on projects with focused objectives. These project teams:

- typically work on a cross-functional (i.e., interdepartmental) challenge or problem;
- are made up of two to six people, usually spanning a natural internal customer-supplier relationship;
- are able to set the team (step 1), clarify the objective (step 2), find the major causes (step 3), and identify the solution (step 4) within six to eight weeks, working approximately two hours per team member per week.

If the team cannot reach the point of developing an action plan to implement the solution within six to eight weeks, then the project scope is too large for a focused CI project team. We are specifically drawing a distinction between a small, focused project and those bigger in scope. Every organization does have some people involved in large-scale projects. Typically, however, the worker level is excluded from project work that creates, innovates, and paves new ground. There always will be a role for broad, large-scope projects. But a great number of improvements can be made by working on small, finite, focused CI projects. And every person in any organization has the capacity to drive the organization forward by getting involved in project teams.

Whether the project is broad and large or finite and focused, the same nine boundary-of-freedom guideposts must be addressed. The boundaries of freedom set for the five moveable guideposts will be reflected in the scope of the project. These boundaries should be established at step 1 in the six-step CI Process.

The five moveable guideposts of boundaries of freedom for CI project teams are supplemented by a specific approach for sorting potential solutions. Sorting solutions into classes serves to reinforce the boundaries of freedom. In the CI Process, solutions are sorted into the following three classes:

- Class 3—Potential solutions that the team determines are *not* practical, feasible, or cost-effective.
- Class 2—Solutions that pass the practical, feasible, and cost-effective test *but* are beyond the project team's boundaries of freedom to act on; these are recommended to a higher authority.
- Class 1—Solutions that are practical, feasible, and cost-effective that are *within* the team's boundaries of freedom; the project team has the authority to act on these.

Employee-Driven Idea Systems

An Employee-Driven Idea System (EDIS) takes the spirit of the traditional suggestion system and adapts it to a TQ environment. EDIS differs from a traditional suggestion system in two basic ways:

1. The employees drive their own idea to completion; the idea (or suggestion) isn't handed over to a committee.
2. It works; an EDIS taps the creative spirit and unleashes the capabilities of the entire organization to make continuous improvement a way of life.

An EDIS is a natural evolutionary step from CI project teams, especially after all know and practice the CI Process. The CI Process works equally well with "teams of one," or individuals, as with formal CI project teams. Step 1, "setting the team," may be simpler, but all other steps are as necessary and valid for an individual formulating, developing, and implementing an idea as for a CI project team.

The same nine boundary-of-freedom guideposts that apply to CI projects apply to employee-driven ideas. However, the actual boundaries should be different under EDIS than with a CI project team.

Work Cells

Work cells dismantle functional barriers. In a work cell, natural internal customers and suppliers in the same work flow (process) are set up next to one another. The work flows naturally, smoothly, and directly from internal supplier to internal customer, who in turn is the internal supplier to the next step in the work flow. Being close to a customer in a work cell gives people the chance to talk, to listen, and to interact. This creates a sense of common purpose and alignment rarely seen in a departmentalized, functional structure. This alignment gives everyone a common desire to improve the linked process, to drive out waste, to get the whole process to work better, smoother, and easier. With alignment, trust follows, and the boundaries of freedom are naturally expanded.

Self-Managed Work Teams

The evolution to self-managed work teams from work cells is a natural step. A self-managed work team is one that manages its own affairs, from hiring and firing to setting a production or work schedule to establishing team goals. Use caution before taking this step, however; it requires a lot of preparation, training, and trust.

An empowered, self-managed work team can be an immensely positive force for an organization. However, there must be a solid history of clear, communicated, and consistently applied boundaries of freedom with two-way ownership of responsibility. Without this foundation, a self-managed work team will not be successful.

Individuals or Teams?: Two Ways to Make Improvements

With our emphasis on teamwork, CI project teams, and work teams, it's easy to forget that employees can make improvements individually, not just in teams. Not every challenge or opportunity for improvement needs more than one person to investigate it, determine the root cause, and develop and implement an action plan. However, the same nine guideposts for setting boundaries of freedom that apply for teams apply for individuals.

The issue at hand is "When do we need a team, and when is one person enough?" The answer, predictably, is, "It depends"; it depends on the limits of the five moveable guideposts as well as the answers to the following five questions (the logic of the five questions is flowcharted in Figure 1.7).

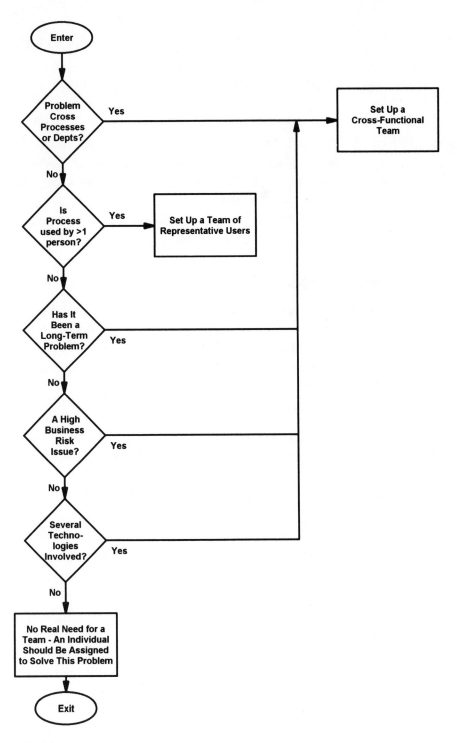

FIGURE 1.7.   Flowchart of Five Questions for Determining if a Team
is Needed

The questions to ask when considering if a team is needed or if an individual can tackle the problem alone are:

1. Does the problem or opportunity for improvement "live" in one process, or does it cross process lines?

   - If the problem or improvement crosses process lines, we have a natural customer-supplier relationship at work; use a cross-functional (cross-process) team.

   - If the problem is contained within one process, it may be a candidate for an individual to work on alone.

2. Do several people, shifts, or departments "use" the process the improvement opportunity lives in?

   - If several people use the process, a representative team of its users should work on the CI team, or, at a minimum, be consulted before an improvement idea is pursued.

   - If only one person works on the process, the improvement opportunity may be a candidate for one person alone.

3. Is it a long-term problem or annoyance?

   - If the problem has been around for a while, a cross-functional team will have a better chance of coming up with a permanent solution than will an individual working alone.

   - If the problem is relatively new, one person may be able to tackle it.

4. Does the problem involve a "high-risk" issue or process? A high-risk issue is one that could create a major morale or safety problem, involves a "life-or-death" business issue, or could adversely impact the external customer base.

   - If the problem or project involves a high-risk issue, a team is better equipped to handle the problem than an individual working alone. A team can see the problem from many perspectives—and a high-risk situation *needs* those viewpoints.

   - If the problem or project doesn't involve a high-risk situation, an individual may be able to tackle it alone.

5. Are technology experts from several different fields needed to effectively work through the problem?

   • If the involvement of experts from several technology fields is needed, a team is necessary by definition.

   • If, however, the technology issues are predominately in one field, one person may be able to tackle the problem or project alone.

The Kaizen *Mine*

The only Japanese term we use in this book is "*kaizen*." Loosely translated, *kaizen* means continuous improvement on top of continuous improvement on top of continuous improvement, or *constant* con-

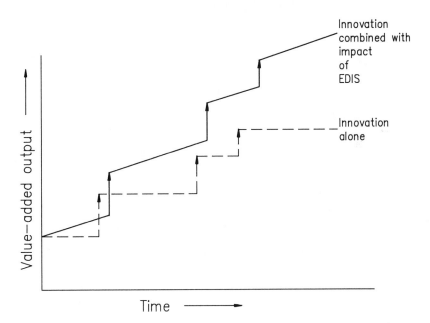

FIGURE 1.8. The Impact of Innovation combined with EDIS Improvements compared with Innovation Alone

(Adapted from *A Practical Guide to Statistical Quality Improvement* by M. R. Beauregard, R. J. Mikulak, and B. A. Olson [N.Y.: Van Nostrand Reinhold, 1992].)

tinuous improvement. When we talk about *kaizen* improvements, we mean small evolutionary improvements as opposed to large revolutionary improvements. The United States is the home of innovation and revolutionary breakthroughs. We recognize and reward the "home-run hitters" in business as well as in baseball. But we don't do as well promoting work on small evolutionary improvements; these are the *kaizen* improvements. All of these small improvements are in what we call the *"kaizen* mine," a gold mine of small improvements, largely untapped in the United States.

An EDIS is the best vehicle we know of to tap that gold. It's driven by empowerment and fueled by recognition. While the big innovative ideas are important, so are the daily *kaizen* improvements. Figure 1.8 shows the difference in overall performance of an organization coupling EDIS improvements (*kaizen*) with innovation compared with one relying on innovation alone.

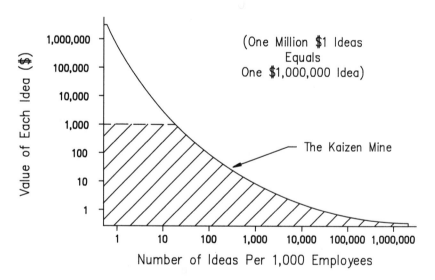

The Kaizen Mine

FIGURE 1.9. The *Kaizen* Mine

(Adapted from *A Practical Guide to Statistical Quality Improvement* by M. R. Beauregard, R. J. Mikulak, and B. A. Olson [N.Y.: Van Nostrand Reinhold, 1992].)

Figure 1.9 provides a conceptual picture of the *kaizen* mine. The premise of the *kaizen* mine is that one million $1 ideas will equal one $1,000,000 idea. There are many more opportunities to come up with ideas that have a $25 or $250 positive net impact on the organization than there are to formulate $250,000-impact ideas. However, if the brainline only allows a select few to think and act to make improvements, the innovative ideas will get most of the attention. With an EDIS in place, all organization members are free to improve their own jobs, and the mother lode of gold in the *kaizen* mine can be tapped.

Summary: Empowerment Through EDIS

Adapt a TQ Process

EDIS and TQM go hand in hand; an EDIS is part of the TQ process. An EDIS will not survive in a traditional, non-TQ environment. To succeed, it must be part of a larger process that focuses on continuous improvement and teamwork through employee involvement.

Create the Environment

The first key element of TQM is Creating the Environment. It's the job of top management; it can't be delegated. It includes developing an empowering Vision that captures the essence of the organization and its future direction, a corresponding set of Guiding Principles, and a TQM Roadmap with tangible and measurable milestones to work the Vision.

Roll Out the CI Toolbox

People need a direction (Vision), but they also need tools to make improvements. The same basic continuous improvement tools necessary to work on CI project teams are needed for an EDIS.

Erase the Brainline

Every organization we've worked with was prey to one of these. Brainlines aren't intentionally put in place; in fact, no one wanted to keep theirs after they realized it existed. To drive it down and out of the organization, acknowledge its existence, and then develop boundaries of freedom so you can begin to get rid of it.

Communicate Boundaries of Freedom

Every one in every job has limits, called boundaries of freedom, to what they can act on. However, if we don't know what our boundary limits are, we aren't free to act—we're paralyzed. Developing and communicating clear, consistent boundaries of freedom is a prerequisite for an EDIS.

Begin CI Projects

Using the CI problem-solving tools in a team is a good way to learn them; applying them to actual projects is a good way to perfect them.

Use the CI Process to Begin an EDIS

An EDIS development team can use the CI process to develop an EDIS for your organization.

Chapter 2

What's Wrong With Traditional Suggestion Systems?

Before we discuss this topic, let's take a look at what we mean by a "traditional" suggestion system. While every suggestion system has unique features, all of them seem to include the following characteristics:

- a focus on financial rewards commensurate with company savings
- limited or restricted eligibility
- little or no involvement by the suggestor in the implementation of the idea

Let's take a look at each of these and how they can slow down or even stop the flow of ideas.

Financial Rewards

By "financial rewards" we mean anything of substantial value, including cash, savings bonds, gift certificates, and merchandise, that is granted to the suggestor of a valid improvement idea. By "commensurate with savings" we mean that the value of the reward is based on the savings the organization should realize as a result of the idea. For example, some organizations "share" the savings with the employees. A common approach is to aware the suggestor 20 percent of the first year's savings. Some companies will continue to compensate the employee for the second year's savings, and some companies go even further than that. Companies that give merchandise instead of cash may award "points" based on savings to the company. Employees can then turn in their points for merchandise or "bank" their points for a larger prize.

Most suggestion systems also have provisions for nontangible awards for those improvements that are difficult to evaluate in terms of savings. For example, let's say an employee has a safety-related idea that may reduce back strains. Since the idea is difficult to measure in terms of direct savings, the employee will receive a fixed-value ($50–$100) award instead. These are typically calculated using a formula that factors in things such as frequency of use of the idea, cost to implement, and the number of people affected by the idea.

The Downside of Financial Rewards

Giving a financial reward makes perfect sense at first glance. After all, if the company is going to save money, why shouldn't it share the savings with the suggestor? It's a great way of recognizing the value of the idea to the company and to encourage others to think up ways to save the company money. But let's take a look at the downside of financial rewards.

First of all, this approach encourages employees to focus on the big ideas because the bigger the idea, the bigger the payback. Smaller ideas that may have limited impact on the organization as a whole, but could result in significant improvement in the quality of an individual's work, may go unrewarded. At best, the employee could receive a nontangible award, but they know that the $50 or so is just a token and not fair compensation compared to the tangible idea. They therefore concentrate their efforts on the big ideas.

In a continuous improvement (CI) environment, we should encourage ideas and participation by everyone regardless of the bottom-line impact. This is, again, known as *kaizen*, the Japanese term for small, continuous, never-ending improvements that build on one another. Our problem in the Western World is that we want instant gratification, immediate payback, big results. We focus our efforts on the home runs, which is exactly what traditional suggestion systems do. They reward people for the home runs and don't give any credit for the single-base hits. Yet how many baseball teams win the pennant because of home runs alone? They are nice to have and sometimes make the difference between winning or losing a game, but in the long run, it's getting on base consistently that wins the season.

If a suggestion system forces employees to focus on big ideas because of the way its rewards are structured, the company may be missing out on hundreds of smaller ideas. In addition, because it's easier to come up with the small ideas than the big ones, there will be significantly less people participating in suggestion systems that encourage only the big ideas.

Financial rewards pose numerous other problems as well. One question a company should ask before implementing a financially based suggestion system is, "How long will this system be in place?" Realistically, it's not going to last forever, at least in the same form. Often, suggestion systems are changed or dropped completely due to financial constraints or a change in management. If you want to see employee improvement ideas come to a dead halt, implement a suggestion system that rewards employees based on the savings to the company and then later cancel it. All of a sudden the ideas will stop, simply dry up. It's the employees' way of telling you that their ideas aren't coming for free. And that makes sense considering the precedent that has been set. Why should someone give an idea today for nothing when, if they had suggested it yesterday, it could have yielded $5,000 or more for them? (An example of converting a traditional reward-based suggestion system to an EDIS is discussed in Chapter 4.)

Another problem with financial rewards is the non–value adding activity of calculating the value of the idea and the award amount. The company, protecting its financial exposure, conservatively estimates the savings. The employee, probably not aware of all of the costs of implementation, overestimates the savings. The dispute begins. Each side is looking out for its own short-term financial interests and no one is focusing on what really matters: How will the improvement help the company over the long term? That's the whole reason for the suggestion system in the first place.

But the biggest problem with a financially based suggestion system is that it discourages teamwork and sends a mixed message to the organization. Where is the incentive for an employee to involve others in refining the idea when he/she will have to share the monetary reward with them? Thus, ideas are not as good as they can be because they generally come from one point of view. Some organizations even formalize this problem by limiting the number of suggestors that can submit an idea.

Limited Eligibility

Many suggestion systems restrict who can or can't submit suggestions. For example, at many companies, only hourly employees are allowed to participate in the suggestion system. Other companies restrict participation to non-exempt employees. Yet another suggestion-system variation restricts submissions to any areas outside of the employees' normal daily responsibilities. All of these approaches seemed logical at the time the organizations developed them, especially since the rewards for ideas were based on savings to the company. After all, salaried employees or exempt personnel typically have jobs with broader scopes and therefore are exposed to more opportunities for improvement. In addition, because of their wider range of responsibility, they are expected to come up with ideas for improvement in the course of their job. "That's what they're paid for," said one company representative.

What kind of message does this send to those people who are eligible to submit suggestions? Could it be the wrong message? Is this type of suggestion system reinforcing the organization's brainline?

In Chapter 1, we discussed that the brainline is that point in the organization that separates those who have to think as a part of their everyday job from those who are told not to think but to do their jobs; they are not expected to make improvements. In a continuous improvement environment, we're constantly pushing the brainline down in the organization, with the goal of driving it out forever. If we start a suggestion system that allows only certain people to participate, we are running the risk that employees will see it as reinforcement of the brainline. In essence, this approach tells eligible employees "We don't expect you to think in your jobs. But, just in case you come up with an idea, we are going to establish a system that will reward you for thinking. Others in the organization aren't eligible because they are expected to think on the job all of the time."

Combine restricted eligibility with financial rewards and you could have some real problems. Some companies have even found that ineligible employees will work together with eligible employees to develop suggestions. Then, the eligible employee submits the idea and shares his/her reward with the ineligible employee. While some may be outraged at this, when you think about it, how, realistically, can an organization that embraces continuous improvement and teamwork fault two employees working together for the good of the company?

Limited Involvement in Implementation

Most traditional suggestion systems simply provide a way for employees to submit their ideas for improvement. The actual implementation of the idea is assigned elsewhere in the organization. Typically, implementation is the job of the engineering department, the maintenance department, or a suggestion committee. Once an employee has submitted his/her idea, he/she is out of the picture (much to the suggestor's dismay). The person or persons responsible for implementing the idea usually harbor some level of resentment toward the suggestor; the suggestion has just caused them extra work. Besides that, the suggestor received some type of financial reward for the idea, whereas the implementor received nothing. The suggestor has the money but no sense of ownership for the idea; he/she resents someone taking responsibility for his/her idea. Typically the implemented solution bears little resemblance to the original idea. The suggestor may be happy with the financial reward but have difficulty in taking pride in the idea without any involvement in its implementation.

Suggestion systems with one, two, or all three of these characteristics are not necessarily bad systems. In fact, many companies have built very successful long-running suggestion programs around these characteristics. But more often than not, they quickly go from suggestion system to rejection system. Battles over how much an idea is worth, who's going to be responsible for implementing the idea, and even just the administrative work involved in keeping such systems going, get in the way of their effectiveness.

In interviewing many employees and companies on their views and concerns about traditional suggestion systems, some common themes emerged. First, we'll look at suggestion systems from the employees' perspective, then the companies'.

The Employees' View of Traditional Suggestion Systems

Only the Big Ideas Are Worth Submitting

Most employees don't consciously suppress small ideas. But because awards are based on savings, they tend to overlook small-improvement opportunities. Safety-related ideas that could help avoid thousands of dollars in worker's compensation costs are difficult to assess, and small ideas that might make it easier for workers to do their job don't register on the suggestion-system award scale. The fact that an injury could be prevented, a life could be saved, or that an employee might be able to produce better quality with a minor modification to the equipment are improvements that are too hard to measure and therefore risky to reward. So after submitting a couple of smaller ideas and being shot down, employees quickly come to realize that the only ideas worth submitting are the big ones.

It Takes Forever for Suggestions to Be Processed

Especially in the early phases of a suggestion program, many ideas come flowing in. It's rare for a company to have a full-time suggestion coordinator, so the burden of processing the suggestions usually falls on the shoulders of a suggestion committee. The members of the suggestion committee are now expected, in addition to their regular responsibilities, to work on processing and implementing other people's ideas even though the ideas may have no direct impact on them. What's in it for the suggestion committee? Not much more than extra work, so the suggestion process slows down to a crawl. To the suggestors, it seems as if their ideas have been thrown into a black hole. Often, that's true. Sometimes, however, the idea is being worked on; it's just not apparent to the suggestor. Behind the scenes, the idea is being analyzed, scrutinized, and evaluated. The suggestion committee is busy ensuring the idea is original—the company wouldn't want to pay an employee for an idea that wasn't his or her own. And they also have to be comfortable that the idea will work—they don't want to pay the employee for an idea that will never be implemented. They have to assure the estimated savings are accurate—they wouldn't want to overcompensate the employee.

Whatever the cause of the delay, what it boils down to in the employee's eyes is that his or her idea is just not that important. As one employee said, "Our ideas are like fine wine—they need time to ferment."

Suggestions Get Lost or Misplaced

A good suggestion-systems administrator won't lose suggestions. Usually, his or her key responsibility is to follow up on ideas and keep them moving through the system. Some have developed elaborate tracking systems that require the suggestion folder (the folder that contains all of the information about the suggestion) be logged in and out through the suggestion administrator before being passed on to the next person. And a good suggestion-systems administrator quickly learns to make copies of all suggestions, just in case the original gets lost. Even with these backups, however, ideas still get lost or misplaced, reinforcing, to the employee, the insignificance of the idea.

Only a Small Number of Suggestions Are Accepted and Implemented

According to the Employee Involvement Association, in 1991 only 33 percent of the suggestions submitted among member companies in the United States were accepted and implemented. That means that an employee has only a one in three chance of having his or her idea accepted. While many of the remaining 67 percent of the ideas are not flat out rejected, they are returned for a variety of reasons, including duplication (the idea has already been submitted by someone else; someone stole my idea!), the process under question is in a state of transition, and therefore, is ineligible for improvement suggestions (I'll hold onto my ideas, then, until they are welcome), it's not cost-effective (it will cost too much), and it's not feasible (it was a really off-the-wall idea).

Some may write off the low 33 percent figure by claiming that 33 percent is better than nothing. Others say it just goes to show the work force isn't very bright. We've even heard one person say that it's a good thing not all ideas are accepted because companies would go broke paying the awards if 100 percent of the ideas were implemented.

The Employee Has Little Say in How an Idea Will Be Implemented

The idea of a traditional suggestion system is to get employees to think up ideas for improvement. Once they submit the idea, their job is done. It's up to someone else to put the idea into action. This takes ownership of the idea away from the suggestor. They have no say in whether it works or not. And, often, the idea the employee submitted and the idea that is implemented are two very different things. By the time the engineers, maintenance personnel, and others get their two cents in, the idea has been improved, modified, scaled down, and expanded beyond the point of recognition. This robs the employee of pride in the suggestion as it is clearly no longer his or her own idea.

The Company's Savings Estimate Is Usually Conservative

Cautious not to overcompensate the employee, estimates of the savings from an idea are conservative. The formula used to calculate the award is difficult to understand and, therefore, difficult to debate. The employee is pretty much stuck with what the company says it

thinks it will save. While some systems provide a grievance proce-
dure if the employee is not satisfied with the award, the employee,
pitted against engineers and accountants, has little power in changing the outcome.

Suggestion Systems Discourage Teamwork

Employees quickly learn that they are best off keeping ideas to themselves. Although they may be able to develop better-quality ideas,
because they know they will have to share the award with the co-
suggestors, they go it alone. Worse yet, if a group of employees is
working together to solve a particular problem and if there's a chance
that the idea will yield big dollar savings, you won't hear about the
idea in the meeting. People will wait until they can submit the idea
as an official suggestion. While the idea was probably the result of
everyone discussing the problem, and without that discussion the
solution would never have been found, one individual still ends up
getting all of the credit and his or her coworkers feel betrayed.

Traditional Systems From
the Company's Viewpoint

No One Has Time to Spend Working on Suggestions

Analyzing and implementing ideas takes a lot of time. Few companies can justify a full-time suggestion-system administrator, so the
task is usually given to a committee on top of its members' regular
daily responsibilities. In addition to regular suggestion meetings,
they must spend non–value adding time checking to assure the idea
is original and that it will save the company money, and overseeing
its implementation. All of this work so the employee can get a financial reward while the suggestion committee members only get the
extra work. As time goes on, the importance of the suggestion system
gets lost in all of the other priorities. Ideas take a backseat to the
tasks committee members are directly accountable for. But as this
happens, the pressure and guilt on committee members increases,

because they know that there are employees depending on their spending time working on suggestions. They wind up resenting the suggestion system and the people making the suggestions.

The Suggestion-System Administrator is Caught in the Middle

Although a part-time or add-on responsibility, someone needs to head the administration of the suggestion system. This person serves as a buffer between the suggestors and the suggestion committee members.

Employees Only Submit Ideas to Make Money

While companies begin suggestion systems usually as a way for employees to participate in making improvements in their work, they quickly come to realize that the reason they get suggestions is because employees are looking to make a little extra money. This reinforces their belief that the only thing that motivates your average worker is the almighty dollar. They have no sense of commitment to the company and take no pride in their work. This just reinforces the us-versus-them mentality, drawing a clear division in the organization, and further entrenching the brainline.

Conclusion

It's clear that although suggestion systems are started with only the best intentions, without a well-thought-out approach, it can backfire on you and you'll actually end up in worse shape than you were before implementing the suggestion system.

As organizations today move toward Total Quality Management and teamwork, it's clear that there needs to be a fresh approach to involving employees in making suggestions for improvement. A poorly designed suggestion system can destroy all the hard work put into a TQM process by sending the wrong message to employees. So if the traditional suggestion system won't work, what will? That's what we'll take a look at in the next chapter.

Chapter 3

What Makes an Employee-Driven Idea System Work?

We've taken a look at why traditional suggestion systems don't work, so now let's see why an Employee-Driven Idea System (EDIS) *will* work. But before we do that, let's look at an example of how one employee used an EDIS to get an idea implemented.

The EDIS Idea Life Cycle

An employee had an idea to install a new type of emergency/safety stop button on his equipment. The new stop button would shut down the equipment and trigger a blinking red light over the machine when it has activated, notifying others in the area of the emergency. To start the idea process rolling, the employee filled out an idea form, and sat down with his supervisor to discuss the idea. Immediately, the supervisor recognized the employee's contribution by thanking him for the idea and giving him an idea coupon worth one dollar.

The employee and supervisor then discussed the idea to determine if it was feasible. This gave the employee a chance to explain the idea in more detail and the supervisor a chance to ask questions. The supervisor approved the idea (in this company, over 80 percent of the ideas are approved), and from there they jointly determined how to proceed.

They decided that the idea would cost $80 to implement. Because the implementation cost for this idea was within the supervisor's approval boundary of $100, he gave the employee the go ahead to implement the idea.

The employee, with the assistance of the supervisor, determined the implementation plan. The installation of the blinking red light required the skills of an electrician. The employee filled out and submitted a work order to the maintenance department. (If the employee had been able to implement the idea on his own, he would have.)

The electrician met with the employee to make sure that he understood what had to be done. Some materials had to be purchased. The employee submitted a requisition for the materials to the purchasing department. (If the purchasing manager had any questions, or if she could not locate the items the employee requested, together they would have worked out an alternate approach.)

The idea was implemented as the employee envisioned. The supervisor followed up with the employee when the idea was implemented and gave him another $1 idea coupon. The employee requested three extra $1 idea coupons from the supervisor to recognize the electrician, the purchasing manager, and the supervisor for helping him.

We've just seen an example of how a typical EDIS works throughout the life cycle of an idea. One thing that we left out is how long it took for the whole process; that's what's really amazing. This idea, from conception to implementation, was handled in two days.

Throughout this example, you no doubt noticed significant differences between the EDIS and a traditional suggestion system. Those differences can be summarized into four major categories:

1. EDIS ideas focus on *kaizen* (small and continuous) improvements.
2. Idea makers maintain ownership of their ideas until they are in place and working.

3. Recognition drives employees to continually improve; financial rewards are not used or are nominal (the dollar coupon).
4. The EDIS reinforces the total quality (TQ) process and teamwork.

In this chapter, we'll look at each of these characteristics in detail.

Kaizen Improvements

In our example, the employee had a small but important idea that would make the workplace safer. The Japanese would call this a *kaizen* idea. While businesses still need innovative breakthroughs, we can't continue to ignore small, everyday improvements.

An EDIS focuses the organization on the "base hits" or the "singles" rather than the one-shot "home run." Each idea moves the organization ahead using small steps. Like the single with runners on base, a small idea from one employee may be the catalyst for improvement in other areas as well. Not only do you get a runner on base, you also get the team to advance as well.

In an EDIS, every now and then there may be a home-run idea, a big one that gets everyone excited and that leads to significant improvement or a giant leap forward. But just like home runs in baseball, in an EDIS they are the exception, not the rule.

Home runs are the exception in a traditional suggestion system too. But since singles and doubles are discouraged, all we see are the home runs. A traditional suggestion system doesn't encourage employees to go for singles. *Kaizen* ideas are squelched.

Some would argue that it takes a long time for all those little ideas (the singles) to amount to anything. But it doesn't take long if we get a lot of ideas. After all, one idea worth $1,000,000 is the same as one-million $1 ideas. The big difference is that the one million $1 ideas lead to one million improvements, not just one. And a lot more people are involved in the process, as against the one $1,000,000 idea that involves just one person. Additionally, the intangible benefits of those million ideas will far surpass the million-dollar mark!

If the one-million $1 ideas don't convince you, maybe a comparison of U.S. and Japanese suggestion systems will. From Table 3.1, you can see that the financial return for adopted ideas is much higher

TABLE 3.1.   A Comparison of U.S. and Japanese
Suggestion Systems (Statistics for 1990)

MEASURE	U.S.	JAPAN
Suggestions per Eligible Employee	0.17	32
Participation Rate	10%	65%
Adoption Rate	33%	87%
Financial Return Per Adoption	$7,102	$129
Financial Return Per Employee	$398	$3,612
Total Suggestions Received	1.5 Million	>50 Million

Source: Michael Verespej, "Suggestion Systems Gain New Luster," *Industry Week*, November 16, 1992, p. 18. (Statistics for 1990.)

in the United States. However, because so many more suggestions are received and implemented in Japan, the bottom-line (average financial return per employee) is that the Japanese *kaizen* approach to suggestion systems works.

Ownership of Ideas

In the blinking red light example, the employee didn't just come up with the idea and drop it in someone else's lap to implement. He managed the implementation of his idea as well. There are several benefits to this approach:

1. It got installed when he wanted it installed, not when someone else got around to it. He wasn't dependent on someone else to get it done for him.
2. He stuck with the installation because he had ownership of the idea throughout the idea life cycle.
3. The idea was implemented as he had envisioned it.

In a traditional suggestion system, once employees make a suggestion, their job is through; it's up to someone else to put the idea into action. (Traditional suggestion systems reinforce the brainline.) The people assigned to implement employee suggestions typically take on that responsibility in addition to all of the other work they have. Since the idea usually isn't that important to the "idea implementors," it is given low priority. So it sits, sometimes for weeks, sometimes for months. The employee has little control over getting the suggestion implemented. This leads to frustration and sends a loud and clear message to all employees that suggestions aren't really that important. In an EDIS, because the employee maintains ownership of the idea, he or she is accountable for its implementation. If the idea isn't installed, the employees have no one to blame but themselves.

Recognition

Immediate recognition occurred throughout the blinking-light example. When the employee submitted the idea, he was recognized by his supervisor. The supervisor again recognized him when the idea was implemented. The employee also had a chance to give recognition to the people who helped him in the maintenance and purchasing departments. The people involved in this idea received constant feedback that what they were doing was important and valuable to the organization; this reinforces teamwork.

A traditional suggestion system's reward structure is counterproductive to a TQ environment. If the employee in our example had been at a company with a traditional suggestion system, the idea probably never would have been submitted; after all, there's no good way to determine how much money the idea could save the company.

He may have informally suggested it to his supervisor, but like most supervisors, he probably would have written it on a small slip of paper and stuffed it in his shirt pocket, never to be seen again. Or perhaps the supervisor would have told him that it wasn't a good idea or that it wouldn't work. For small ideas, employees get no recognition and no reward. Worse yet, something they felt was important fell on deaf ears. In any case, if that happens two or three times, employees will eventually get the message that their ideas aren't really welcome or wanted.

Total Quality and Teamwork

In the blinking-light example, the employee worked with people in other departments to get his idea implemented. Why were people so helpful to him? Why doesn't this happen in a traditional suggestion system?

A traditional suggestion system places large demands on everyone involved in the process, yet the only hero is the suggestor. He or she is the only person who is rewarded or recognized for the suggestion. This creates resentment from others who helped the suggestor when he gets a check and they get nothing. This resentment eventually leads to a breakdown in teamwork. Everyone starts looking out for themselves. Secrecy, not teamwork, is built into the environment. People begin to think, "Why should I take my time helping someone else make a profit with their suggestions?"

Teamwork between suggestors also suffers in a traditional suggestion system. Employees will not share their ideas with others for fear they will have to split the suggestion reward money. While one employee may have a good idea, it could turn into a great idea if it was discussed with coworkers before being submitted. This rarely happens in a traditional suggestion system, however; it's every man for himself.

An EDIS is structured to recognize the interdependency of everyone in the organization. Idea makers know that without the help of others, their ideas would never come to fruition. This reinforces the TQ philosophy and enhances teamwork.

Conclusion

An EDIS represents a radical departure from the traditional suggestion system. Table 3.2 shows a comparison between a traditional suggestion system and an EDIS.

Today's TQ environment requires us to think about employee

TABLE 3.2. A Comparison of an Employee-Driven Idea System and a Traditional Suggestion System

Characteristic	*EDIS*	*Traditional Suggestion System*
Type of ideas	Small *Kaizen* idea focused on improving the employees' work area	Large, innovative idea focused on improving a nagging problem
"Reward system"	Immediate recognition for both submitting an idea and for implementing the idea	Share in the first one or two years' financial savings
Approval of the idea	Primarily the supervisor's responsibility	The suggestion committee's responsibility
Timing of idea approval	Quick, measured in days, sometimes hours	Slow, measured in weeks, sometimes months
Linkage to a TQ process	Complements and integrates well with a TQ environment	The antithesis of a TQ approach
Implementation of ideas	Employees manage and implement their own ideas	The suggestion committee plans for the implementation of the idea. The employee has little input on implementation
Teamwork	Encouraged when ideas cross functions or when they are large	Discouraged because the employee will have to share the financial reward with others
Administration time	Minimal administration time is required	An elaborate administration system is needed to track ideas

ideas in a different way. No longer are employee ideas something unexpected for which they must be compensated. They should be expected. They are needed for the good of everyone in the organization. The traditional suggestion system cannot give us the speed of response and flexibility required to put employee ideas to work on a daily basis. An EDIS is the only way to capture employee ideas, recognize their contributions, and track results in a formal way without bureaucracy or nonvalue-adding work.

Chapter 4

Recognition or Rewards?

Many people use the two words recognition and rewards inter-
changeably. We define them to be two significantly different things:

- Rewards involve tangible, material, or financial compensation.
- Recognition involves acknowledging contributors and accomplishments by letting contributors know what they have done is important and has made a difference.

Recognition over Rewards

We link our definitions to the work of Frederick Herzberg and his
motivator-hygiene theory of work motivation.[1] Herzberg divides factors or needs affecting individual work drive into two general categories: hygiene needs and motivator factors.

The hygiene factors for work include those elements that provide
a healthy, stable work environment, such as pay, security, and safe-

---

[1]Frank J. Landy and Dan A. Trumbo, *Psychology of Work Behavior* (Home-
wood, IL: Dorsey Press, 1976), p. 302.

ty. We place tangible, material, or financial "rewards" in the hygiene needs category.

We place "recognition" in the motivator factor class. According to Landy and Trumbo in *Psychology of Work Behavior*, motivator factors or needs are "related to some innate characteristic of individuals which require them to seek challenge, stimulation, and autonomy. These needs are satisfied by things such as responsible work, independence of action, and recognition for the accomplishment of difficult tasks."

Herzberg proposes that once work-hygiene needs have been satisfied, motivators are more important to individuals than additional hygiene satisfiers. We agree. Simply put, there is a point of diminishing return using pay as a motivator.

In accordance with this view, we make one basic assumption about pay or compensation and one basic assumption about motivation in our separation of rewards and recognition:

1. Compensation assumption—We assume that employees receive pay that is fair and equitable (i.e., that the hygiene need of pay is met at an acceptable level).
2. Motivational assumption—We assume that we cannot affect the internal motivation of employees; we can only create an environment in which they motivate themselves.

If the compensation assumption holds for any given organization, we must then look to recognition, not rewards, as the ongoing catalyst of an Employee-Driven Idea System (EDIS). Table 4.1 summarizes our observations.

Recognition Is the Catalyst

We are not proposing that recognition alone is the sole catalyst for an EDIS. But most organizations have handled recognition poorly in the past. Adoption of a sincere, timely recognition approach will be a powerful driver of an EDIS in the early stages. Over time, after perhaps two or three years, it will become necessary to share the financial gains an EDIS brings to organizations. (We'll discuss the addition of a *gainsharing* system later in this chapter.) But we must reinforce the idea that recognition is the catalyst of an EDIS; sharing of finan-

TABLE 4.1. Relationship Between Recognition Emphasis and Rewards Emphasis

RECOGNITION	Emphasized	This approach reinforces rugged individualism, hurts teamwork.	This is an environment on a TQ process track.
	Downplayed	This is the way a traditional suggestion system works.	This is a closed environment, not open to new ways or new ideas.
		Emphasized	Downplayed
		FINANCIAL REWARDS($)	

cial gains eventually will boost the EDIS, but should never be the catalyst or the motivator.

Why Do We Recognize?

In the last section we offered a motivational premise: We cannot affect the internal motivation of employees; we can only create an environment in which they motivate themselves. As you'll recall from Chapter 1, Creating the Environment is the first of the three key elements of Total Quality Management; Creating the Environment is the role of (top) management.

Creating the Environment includes:

1. Developing an empowering Vision that points the way to the future of the organization.
2. Providing a clear set of Guiding Principles so everyone knows the fundamental values and beliefs of the organization.
3. Creating a TQM Roadmap with measurable and tangible steps or milestones needed to work the Vision.
4. Establishing and communicating clear, consistent boundaries of freedom that enable employees to take action within their prescribed boundaries.
5. Adoption of performance measures and compensation methods that build, not tear down, teamwork.

These five management (better phrased as leadership) activities go a long way toward creating an environment in which employees will motivate themselves. They will be empowered:

- to think of new ways to improve their work;
- to act, put their ideas into place;
- to innovate, and do what before was not doable;
- to delight their customers, both internal and external.

Positive Feedback

When self-motivated employees initiate or implement an idea, they need and deserve positive feedback (or recognition). Management should acknowledge that:

- *they are doing the right things.* Reinforce the idea that the employee is doing the right thing by acting on the right to initiate and/ or implement ideas. This will further clarify the boundaries of freedom.
- *they are doing things right.* Reinforce the idea that employees are supposed to take action to make improvements, even if the improvement seems to be small in the grand scheme of things. The organization needs improvements from every corner. Only when everyone adopts an attitude to continuously improve everything will the organization be assured of being a "winner" for the long haul.

Giving positive feedback (recognition) to someone for initiating or implementing an idea, even those that lead to seemingly small improvements, reinforces the kind of action we want to encourage in every organization. Expectation of positive feedback will cause others to model the actions of the idea initiator or implementor; after all, we all want to receive positive strokes. Continuous improvement has a snowballing effect, compounding and building upon itself to improve the organization's performance, making it a winning organization. And more will join in; after all, we all want to be part of a winning team.

TABLE 4.2. The Three Stages of an EDIS

Stage	The Focus	Relative Timeline
One	Increasing the participation in the generation of ideas	Two to three years from the start of an EDIS (before moving to stage two)
Two	Improving the value-adding impact of the ideas	After stage one, an organization should spend two to five years before moving to stage three
Three	Increasing the economic impact of the ideas	An organization may be ready for stage three four or more years after beginning an EDIS

When is Enough Enough?

As discussed in Chapter 3, an EDIS will evolve and mature over time. Stage one (the first year or two) focuses on increasing participation in generating ideas, lots of ideas (see Table 4.2). The level of positive feedback is a major influence on the level of participation. Stage two of an EDIS involves additional training directed at increasing the value-adding impact of ideas. In stage three of an EDIS, the emphasis shifts or evolves to increasing the economic impact on the organization.[2]

As the EDIS evolves, so does the positive feedback, or recognition, approach. No, we don't withhold recognition at any time, but we do evolve the recognition methodology to make sure recognition is both appropriate and sincere.

We must return to the basic question of this section: *why* do we recognize? We recognize for action that delights! We have had many company presidents tell us they would be delighted if their people

---

[2]Masaaki Imai, *Kaizen: The Key to Japan's Competitive Success* (New York: Random House, 1986), p. 113.

took initiative, came up with any new idea, and acted on it. So it is early in the evolution of an EDIS; management will be "delighted" when employees begin to initiate ideas, any ideas. "Delight" will be in the air again when idea initiators implement their ideas. But over time, some of the things that initially delight will *come to be expected*; they will no longer be cause for "delight" or recognition. And so begins the evolution of the EDIS.

Three Levels of Response and Chicken Soup

In general, there are three levels of response to any transaction:

- Expected
- Requested
- Delighted

We'll look first at how these three responses apply to "chicken soup" and then relate them back to recognition and an EDIS. Let's say one day, around lunchtime, you decide to try that old greasy-spoon diner down the street you've always wondered about but never had the stomach to try. You sit down and check the menu. Nothing really looks good but you're here and feel obligated to order something. You figure no one can ruin chicken soup, so you order a bowl. At $1.45, you don't expect much, you're just hoping not to get indigestion. Imagine your surprise when the bowl of soup is served, and it's *huge*, has lots of chunks of carrots, celery, and real chicken, comes with a freshly baked loaf of french bread, and everything is delicious! You're delighted!

When you ordered the bowl of soup, you *requested* it. You requested (or specified) a bowl, not a cup, filled with chicken soup, not clam chowder. You didn't *request* the soup be hot, you *expected* it to be served hot. Likewise, you didn't request it be served without flies swimming in it (even though you thought about it); you *expected* it to be "fly free." When you received the soup and the french bread, you were *delighted*! The meal exceeded your *expectations*. You were so pleased with the soup that the next week, you visited the diner again and ordered chicken soup.

Now your *expectations* are raised. You don't expect to get indigestion, you expect a pretty good bowl of soup. When the soup you *request* is again served in a huge bowl, full of chunks of vegetables and chicken with a fresh loaf of french bread, you're *delighted* once again. However, on week three, when you once again visit the diner for chicken soup, you now *expect* the same huge bowl of soup with the loaf of bread. *What once delighted is now expected.* The switch from delighted to expected happens all of the time, and it happens quickly. There is nothing wrong with it, it's natural; it's all part of continuous improvement.

Recognition Changes Over Time

The switch from *delighted* to *expected* in an EDIS occurs just like it does with chicken soup. It's part of the evolution of an EDIS. The level and type of recognition that is appropriate will change over time. We don't recognize people for the same actions over and over. The unexpected action that delighted will become the routine if we build the improvement into the process. We don't stop recognition but we change the form to one that is appropriate for "routine" action. (We'll discuss forms of recognition later in this chapter.)

When Do We Recognize?

When do we recognize? This question is a no-brainer. We all know the answer—it's *fast*, as in immediately. Nothing ages as poorly as an opportunity for recognition. The opportunity half-life is measured in hours. Wait a day and much of the impact of the recognition is lost. Wait a week, and the praise rings weak and hollow. Wait a month, and we feel a need to embellish an act that is actually weakened by the embellishment.

Recognize people for actions that delight with *speed*, as close to the occurrence of those actions as possible. Do it in person, face to face. It's good to reinforce the immediate recognition later by note or memo, in a department or companywide meeting, or in a newsletter. But don't replace face-to-face recognition with written acknowledgment; written acknowledgment doesn't carry the same punch. When you offer recognition to someone face to face, you let them know

TABLE 4.3. Relationship Between Speed of Recognition and Sincerity of Recognition

		Insincere	Sincere
SPEED	Fast	In this environment, it's not recognition, it's really lip service.	This is an environment on a TQ process track.
	Slow	This combination reinforces the brainline.	In this situation, the rate of idea submissions will fall off over time.
		Insincere	Sincere
		SINCERITY	

that they are important (you spent time on them) and their actions were important too (important enough for your individual attention). Table 4.3 summarizes our observations on the relationship between the *speed* of recognition by managers and their sincerity.

Two Speed Demons

Two organizations with a well-established EDIS are Milliken & Company and Toyota Motor Manufacturing U.S.A., Inc. Speed of recognition of ideas is built into their suggestion systems.

- Milliken has a "24-72 rule" about their suggestion system, called the Opportunity for Improvement (OFI) program. Acknowledgment (recognition) of suggestions must be made within 24 hours of the suggestion's submittal, and disposition of the suggestion (its eventual fate) must be made and communicated within 72 hours.[3]

- At Toyota Motor Manufacturing U.S.A., Inc., supervisors are trained to provide *immediate* recognition to the idea generators. They make each employee feel that his or her idea is important. In many cases, the supervisor can also approve the idea on the spot.

---

[3]Carla Kalogeridis, "Milliken in motion: A pursuit of excellence," *Textile World* (December 1990).

Recognition Goes Two Ways

Too often we only think of recognition as a one-way street, with managers recognizing their employees for actions that delighted the manager. But a TQ organization is a learning organization. In a learning organization, everyone, including managers, are continuously learning so they can find new ways to improve the organization. Managers need recognition for actions that delight (their employees) too.

Fast, face-to-face recognition does not come naturally. In fact, most managers have never been trained in (positive) recognition methodologies. Managers have gotten where they are by being good at looking for what's wrong and quickly and effectively responding to problems, not by looking for what's right. Recognition involves looking for what employees do right and acknowledging those actions. When managers learn and practice new, positive recognition skills, they have earned recognition too—from their managers and their employees. If we want our managers to continue to practice this newly learned skill, we have to let them know that they are doing the right thing and doing things right.

Who Do We Recognize?

Who to recognize may seem like a simple, straightforward question, but it's not. Let's look at some of the complications. Should we recognize:

- all idea initiators (we call the initiators the "idea makers")? Or should we recognize only those with the "good" ideas?
- the person (the "idea coach") who helped the idea maker formulate the idea?
- the "idea manager," the one who coordinates the idea implementation?
- those who helped the idea manager implement the idea (the "idea installers")?

The answer to all the complicating questions is *yes!* All involved in the idea deserve recognition, although the form of recognition may differ from role to role.

Four Roles in an EDIS

An EDIS has four distinct roles:

1. Idea maker
2. Idea manager
3. Idea installer
4. Idea coach

Idea Maker

The idea maker is the idea initiator, or the person who came up with the idea.

Idea Manager

The idea manager coordinates implementation of the idea. The idea manager brings the idea from concept to reality.

Idea Installer

The idea installer(s) helps the idea manager implement or put the idea into action.

The Idea Coach

The idea coach is typically the idea maker's supervisor but could be any manager who helps facilitate the idea and steers the idea manager through the tangle of red tape he/she may encounter.

One Person, Three Roles

Ideally, the idea maker is also the idea manager and the idea installer. Early in the evolution of an EDIS, this will not be the case. At first, not all idea makers will have the training and confidence to be idea managers; they'll be more comfortable turning the implementation of their ideas over to others. In some cases, ideas will be large or involve specialized skills or knowledge. The idea managers will need help from others when implementing the idea. Those bringing additional skills or assistance to the idea implementation are the idea installer(s) who may be one individual or a team. So with some ideas, the idea maker, manager, and installer will be the same person. With other ideas, the idea maker will pass the idea on to the idea manager, who will seek the assistance of an idea installer to get the idea implemented.

Recognize to Build Teamwork

Don't use recognition schemes to set up competition between employees, departments, or divisions. Recognize all good things that happen, not only the "best." When we set up a competition it may seem like all are working hard to "win," but in fact the organization becomes the loser.

If We Share Our Ideas With Them, They May Get Ahead of Us

In a competition, a "us-versus-them" attitude is encouraged, or so it seems. People won't help their "competitors" for fear of helping themselves become the loser!

Their Ideas Aren't Worthy of Our Department

Ideas implemented effectively in one department may be resisted in another. As competition builds, the NIH (not invented here) syndrome gets stronger and stronger. NIH is common in business today. It needs to be driven out, not reinforced. Every person and every department should embrace, not reject, the ideas of others in the organization. Think of how much faster your organization could improve and grow if it didn't spend so much time reinventing the wheel.

The Idea Support Team

Implemented ideas are the culmination of the input and activity of many sources. The idea maker is the person who summarized and crystallized the idea. He or she often receives inspiration for the idea from others. The idea manager (who is often the idea maker) may receive help from idea installer(s) as well as several other support people (e.g., from maintenance, data processing, accounting, or warehouse departments). The idea coach empowers the idea maker with redirection (if needed), approval, and facilitation. When an idea is put in place, the entire idea support team, from the idea maker through the idea coach, deserves some level of recognition for helping implement the idea. We'll discuss some ways to share recognition later in this chapter, but first let's look at an example of what we mean by the idea support team.

An Idea and Its Support Team

In 1992, an hourly production worker at Quantum, a division of Chromalloy Gas Turbine Corporation located in Wallingford, CT, came up with a simple, but brilliant, idea that saved Quantum tens of thousands of dollars a year. Entrapped air bubbles (voids) had plagued the urethane casting department for over 11 years. Rework was the only way they knew to fix the problem despite the many hours of engineering time that had been invested to solve the problem during the years. A team of hourly workers was formed. Using basic CI tools, the team determined the voids were trapped when the part was molded. Recalling her grandmother tapping a cake on the table to get out air bubbles before baking it, one woman recommended a similar solution to the manufacturing manager. The idea worked; it solved the problem!

When we tell the story, we're usually asked: "Did the woman get a bonus for her idea?" No, she didn't get a bonus (or a reward). After all, she didn't come up with the idea in a vacuum. Her teammates used CI tools to identify the problem, the manufacturing manager acted as her idea coach, and the maintenance department installed the idea. What the woman did get was something worth more to her. She was recognized by management and her peers:

- as the idea maker;
- as someone who made a difference;
- as an important member of the idea support team.

Although she came up with the idea, she needed help from her supervisor to put the idea into action. Her supervisor became not only the idea coach but also the idea manager in this case. Implementation required the talents of a mechanic, and several other production operators—all idea installers. The entire idea support team received recognition for its role in the idea's success.

Quantum management's recognition showed the young idea maker that she was a catalyst allowing Quantum to improve its products and services. Because of this improvement the company also dramatically increased its market share. Do you think the recognition she received had an impact on her self-image and self-esteem? You bet; she now feels like an important member of the Quantum team. Although, she doesn't hold the title of manager, nor is she a design engineer, she is a valued member of the Quantum team. What's the value of recognition? Money can't buy the impact it will have on your organization.

Recognition Is Not a Finite Commodity

We all know people who can't be happy for other people's success. They withhold congratulations or praise. It's as if they think that if they hand out praise to someone else, there will be less left for them.

The same thing happens with recognition in the work place. Some supervisors and managers are reluctant to recognize employees because they see recognition as a finite commodity. Their actions imply that there is only so much recognition they can pull out of the "recognition jar," and when it's empty, it can never be filled again. They work hard at saving every morsel of recognition for "special" actions.

There are some obvious problems with this approach. If recognition is infrequently given and slow and/or insincere when it is doled out, it will be in limited demand. Most people (employees) will stop doing things they don't receive positive feedback for; they'll stop initiating and implementing ideas if recognition doesn't reinforce they are doing the right things.

Recognition shouldn't be withheld. It is a limitless commodity when used appropriately, promptly, and sincerely. And as recognition is used more and more, the opportunities for additional recognition will multiply.

How Do We Recognize?

Say Thank You Several Ways

Recognition is saying thank you. Acknowledging an idea maker for initiating an idea or an idea manager for implementing an idea by letting them know they have "done the right thing" and "done it right" is thanking them. But different people hear and receive thank-yous in different ways. For some, a private, in-person thank-you recognition is the most effective. For others, thank-you recognition in front of a group (their peers, the management team, or even the whole organization) is the ultimate reward. Do both but don't stop there. Back up the face-to-face thank-yous in print with a personal, informal note, a bulletin-board acknowledgment, or in the company newsletter. There are many, many ways to say thank you, but *always* start with face-to-face recognition—it's the core—and then add to it.

Different Strokes for Different Folks

It would be great if there was one formula for recognizing employees that would work every time. Research on what motivates people has been a favorite topic of industrial psychologists for decades, but much of the research has ignored the fact that different people respond to recognition differently. Recognition is a personal thing; how you approach it depends on the person being recognized. Carl Jung's theory of psychological type, which was further developed and put into a user-friendly form by Isabel Myers and Catherine Briggs,[4] can provide insight into why people respond differently to recognition and appreciation. Myers and Briggs, the mother-daughter team who

---

[4]Isabel B. Myers and Mary H. McCaulley, *A Guide to the Development and Use of the Myers-Briggs Type Indicator* (Palo Alto, CA: Consulting Psychologists Press, 1985).

developed the Myers-Briggs Type Indicator, identified 16 distinct personality types based on the way people perceive things, make judgments about things, and how they interact with the world.

Among other categories, Myers and Briggs classify people as either thinking or feeling people. Thinking or feeling refers to the way people make decisions or judgments. People who prefer thinking tend to be logical, detached, analytical, and driven by objective reasoning. Those who prefer feeling on the other hand, make subjective, value-driven decisions based on how others will feel about the decision. Ask each type how they like to be appreciated or recognized and the differences are glaring. Table 4.4 shows the differences between the two.

TABLE 4.4. Differences in Recognizing Thinking and Feeling People

	Thinking People	*Feeling People*
Who do you like to be recognized by?	Peers, superiors, someone who's successful that I respect	Everyone
What do you like to be recognized for?	Competence, abilities, vision, accomplishments, getting the job done, innovation, creativity	Being useful and helpful, assisting others, upholding ethical standards
How do you like to be recognized?	Concise words and in the presence of others	Many words, gifts, touch
How often do you need recognition?	Only when it's deserved for a substantial contribution	Frequently, even for small things
What happens when you're not appreciated?	Rationalize why the recognition was not deserved. Try harder next time, but will eventually give up or go elsewhere.	Lose confidence and become depressed and angry.

The dynamics of psychological type multiply when you consider that not only do we have to consider the employee's (the recognition recipient) type but also the type of the person giving the recognition. For example, a manager who has a strong preference for thinking over feeling may be way off track when recognizing an employee with a preference for feeling. The manager may focus his words on how the employee's contribution has impacted the company in terms of efficiency, while the employee is looking for strokes about how he has made everyone's job easier.

This short section on the Myers-Briggs is not intended to make you competent at identifying the personality types of the people you work with. Rather, it's to heighten your awareness that different people respond differently to different types of recognition. Be aware of this as you develop a recognition system or as you are personally recognizing someone. If you don't get the response you expected from the employee at first, don't give up, muttering under your breath about how ungrateful the coworker is; instead, try a different angle.

Our purpose in discussing the Myers-Briggs is to point out that we need to recognize different people differently. You can learn more about how the Myers-Briggs can be used in a business setting by contacting The Association for Psychological Type, Kansas City, Missouri.

Always Be Sincere

Don't use "standard phraseology." The entire management team at one organization we worked with had been using the same tired, rote phrase to supposedly "recognize" people. It was a joke; people listened quietly and tried not to laugh as their boss mumbled the same meaningless words; good intentions but bad execution.

Instead of a prepared phrase, explain the impact the idea had on the organization, specifically relating how the action helped make the organization better. Sincere words linked to the reality of the situation are better than any prepared text.

But make sure your message is received correctly. Although it may seem odd, sometimes an employee may expect to be reprimanded and hears a complaint when it's really a compliment. Make sure the face-to-face recognition session is long enough to watch the employee's body language and check to see that a positive stroke, not a reprimand, was received.

Recognition and Celebration Go Hand in Hand

We recognize individuals and teams. A public celebration gives others a chance to say thank you and to commemorate the improvements and benefits everyone will get from the idea.

Recognizing Individuals

There are many individuals to be recognized once an idea has been initiated and implemented. Look at the time and effort it takes to recognize individuals not as a burden, but as an opportunity to invest in the EDIS and to multiply the number of new ideas. Chapter 5 offers suggestions for recognizing the idea maker, the idea manager, idea installer(s), and the idea coach. Scorecards, recognition coupons, and bonus coupons for achieving certain milestones are discussed.

Recognizing Groups

Recognition that singles out one person or even one department as the best can destroy teamwork. It doesn't build teamwork among employees and between departments when the stakes are high. Instead, recognize the entire organization for events such as achieving 75 percent participation, 1,000 ideas in one year, an 80 percent idea-implementation rate, reducing the turnaround time from idea initiation to implementation, and topping five ideas per person on average for the year. All events such as those listed are great excuses for celebration. And public celebrations are opportunities for peer recognition.

Peer Recognition

Recognition of peers by peers cannot replace recognition by management. However, it is additive. A peer recognition committee (discussed in Chapter 5) is an effective way to formalize peer recognition.

A peer recognition committee can select the "top" ideas of a time period, usually a quarter. When a committee of peers select the top ideas of the quarter, it's not received the same way as management choosing the top ideas would be. When management tries to select the top ideas, it never comes off in a positive light; there are too many "losers," with the EDIS being the biggest loser.

The peer recognition committee can operate as a subcommittee of the TQM Council. The TQM Council needs to set clear boundaries of freedom for the committee. It's a good idea to include rotating membership as part of the boundaries. Membership rotation prevents any semblance of favoritism and assures that the committee will continually gain fresh perspectives. A peer recognition committee should be fairly large. A group of 10 employees should assure a good cross section of the organization.

Some Forms of Recognition

Below we list a potpourri of simple, tested recognition methods. There is no need to adapt all of them, except for the first one, face-to-face recognition. In fact, it is best not to use them all, at least at the same time. Recognition processes should be dynamic and changing and be re-energized from time to time. Use the approaches that work for your organization. What works for some organizations (or work cultures) won't for others. However, keep in mind that what doesn't seem to work today may be right tomorrow.

Face-to-Face Recognition

Face-to-face recognition is the most powerful and important form of recognition, but in some ways, it's also the toughest for managers to do. Managers and supervisors haven't been taught to be nurturing, and most are uncomfortable with this role.

$1, a Lottery Ticket, or a $1 Coupon
Token of Appreciation

It's not really the $1 that's important; it's the personal attention "from above" that all cherish. The $1 token is just a way to create the discipline to do it, to make that walk and talk to the idea maker or idea manager face to face and tell them "You've done well!" This inexpensive token of appreciation is a common thread of many of the successful EDIS's we've studied in both Japan and the United States.

Thank-You Notes

We were all told by our parents to write thank-you notes for gifts or acts of kindness. But how many of us still do? An informal, short, handwritten, sincere thank-you note takes minutes to write. Two or three sentences is all that's needed, yet it's impact can last for years. In *Thriving On Chaos*,[5] 1987, Tom Peters reports:

> Sam Preston recently retired as executive vice president of S. C. Johnson (Johnson Wax, etc.). He had a habit of sending little notes, with a bold "DWD" scrawled across the top, after coming across a sparkling effort. The "DWD" stands for "Damned Well Done." At his retirement party, Preston was stunned. People came up and thanked him for DWDs sent fifteen years before. Recognition is that memorable and that infrequent (p. 308).

Peters cites another example of recognition and thank-you notes:

> Consider a ritual like that of the top property manager of Marriott's in Albuquerque, New Mexico. He makes it a rigorous habit to send out at least 100 thank-you notes a month to his staff for jobs well done. You don't think you can find a hundred things worth saying thank you for? That's a prime indicator that you are out of touch (p. 309).

An EDIS Recognition Center

Start an EDIS recognition center. Use a centrally located, highly visible bulletin board (perhaps in the lunch room) to publicize the idea-maker scorecard, the participation-rate thermometer, announcements, pronouncements, and general good news of ideas and improvements and successes. It works best if it's kept up by an EDIS

---

[5]Tom Peters, *Thriving on Chaos* (New York: Knopf, 1987).

communication subcommittee, not by the management team. (You'll find more on the recognition center in Chapter 5.)

Gold Stars

It may sound silly to talk about gold stars; didn't they go out in third grade? But gold stars do work. Some college football teams use "stars" (actually, football stickers placed on helmets) to recognize players who make significant contributions to the team. The stars are worn proudly and serve as an inspiration to others. The associates at a major discount chain receive gold stars for exceptional customer service. The stars are worn on their name tag for their peers and customers to see. However, the stars are given for achieving a milestone, not for winning a competition. Competitions have winners, but mostly they have losers; milestone achievements only have winners, and there isn't a maximum to the number of winners.

Hall (or Wall) of Fame

The hall of fame is a larger version of the bulletin board. It takes up an entire hallway or wall. It gives you more room for plaques, photographs, and other recognition vehicles related to the EDIS.

Casual Days

One large insurance company celebrates with a casual day once a month. The standard dress code calls for a business suit. On the first Friday of each month, anyone who submitted an idea the previous month can dress down in blue jeans and sports shirts or blouses. Most people who work in an office environment relish the opportunity to wear more comfortable attire; it is an effective recognition vehicle that costs nothing. It's a stimulus to increase participation as well. A quick glance is all that's needed to see who submitted an idea and who didn't; talk about peer pressure!

Company Newsletters

Company newspapers are a natural place for reinforcing recognition, but shouldn't be used as the primary vehicle of recognition.

Local Newspapers

Local newspapers are a great place to add high visibility to EDIS progress and significant milestones such as a 75 percent participation rate or reaching an average of five ideas per employee in a year.

Coffee and Donuts or Pizza and Soda Breaks

Organization- or site-wide coffee and donut or pizza and soda breaks are not inexpensive compared with some other forms of recognition, but they are relatively inexpensive special treats to celebrate major EDIS milestones.

A Barbecue

An alternative to pizza and soda is a site-wide barbecue, not catered, but with the managers and supervisors doing the cooking and serving. Managers and supervisors do the cooking not to save caterer fees, but to serve those that fuel the CI journey.

Expanding Boundaries of Freedom

An often overlooked but major recognition vehicle is expanding boundaries of freedom. Expanding the boundaries of the five moveable guideposts is one of the highest forms of recognition an individual or team can receive. It means they have earned greater trust, broader authority, and more autonomy through their past performance.

Basic EDIS Recognition Guidelines

We've discussed several forms of recognition, so before we move on to the exploration of reward systems, let's recap the essential recognition elements of any EDIS.

1. Recognize the idea maker for each and every idea.
2. Do not differentiate recognition based on the potential (economic) value of the idea; recognize all ideas equally.
3. Recognize the idea manager, even if the idea manager and the idea maker are the same person.

4. Don't forget to recognize the idea installer(s) and the idea coach.

5. Set up recognition approaches as win-win, not win-lose; don't create a competition among people or groups for recognition. Competition between people creates losers.

6. Instead of competition between groups, set organizationwide milestones to shoot for.

7. Keep the recognition-system dynamic. Change it over time to re-energize the EDIS to keep up with the changing needs of the work force.

8. Include a peer-recognition component in the recognition methodology. Set boundaries of freedom for the peer recognition committee; don't dictate its approach.

9. Always include face-to-face as part of the recognition scheme.

Why Not Use Rewards?

We've focused on recognition not rewards this entire chapter. And we've repeatedly admitted that face-to-face recognition is not something most managers know how to do well or enjoy doing. So why not just give in and use some material form of reward instead? It would be a lot easier.

Material rewards are easier to give out than spending the mental and emotional energy on sincere recognition. You may reason that rewards don't have to be big-ticket items; passes to the movies, gift certificates to a restaurant, or even $10 or $20 bills aren't going to break the bank, are they? And people like those tangible rewards, too, don't they? They sure do, but let's look at what happens if we tie EDIS recognition to material rewards or prizes.

Who Decides?

How do we decide which reward to give? If material rewards or prizes are used, more than one type will probably find its way into use. Who decides which reward or prize goes to whom? Should the idea maker get a different reward than the idea installer? Should the idea installer who spent one day helping with the idea get a bigger prize than the idea installer who spent one hour?

The administrative time and energy spent keeping the reward records straight (and the inventory of prizes current) will detract attention from the real objectives of an EDIS.

The "You Owe Me" Cycle

When prizes are used to recognize ideas or implementation action, people will begin linking prizes to the value-adding impact of their ideas on the organization. It's only natural for people to begin to think, "I gave you (the company) this (idea), now you (the company) owe me (the idea maker) something (of commensurate value) in return." We call this the "you owe me" cycle.

It usually starts when a person has an idea with large positive impact on the organization. They may say something to the effect of, "Robin got two movie tickets for her idea. Mine is worth a whole lot more than her's. Shouldn't I get at least four tickets?" And the "you owe me" cycle is put in place.

Prizes Forever?

If prizes are given out, won't people continue to expect prizes for doing the same things forever?

Remember the three levels of response (discussed earlier in this chapter): expected, requested, and delighted. Even with an EDIS, we don't continue to recognize every type of action forever. As long as the affected system is changed to incorporate the improvements involved, action that once delighted will become part of the expected. It's easy to adjust recognition systems but it's tough to change, as in "take away," prizes or rewards.

What Happens If We Forget Someone?

Any time we recognize (or reward) for an action, probably more than one person has been involved in the activity. Almost any idea has an entire idea support team helping bring it to life. What happens if we forget to recognize someone on the support team? It's not good, but it's even more difficult to recover when prizes are used and someone is left out.

Bigger and Bigger Prizes?

With a prize system, the tendency is to add bigger and bigger prizes. Two tickets to a movie will become four and then a booklet of ten. A $10 gift certificate to a local restaurant will become a $50 dinner for two. The value of the prize can spiral upward until someone says "Enough!" and puts an end to the rewards. Then management will wonder why the steady stream of ideas has suddenly dried up.

Gainsharing Makes Sense

At some point, the addition of tangible, financial rewards to intangible recognition does make sense. However, the timing and the approach have to be right, continuing to add value to the EDIS evolution. Gainsharing is sharing a portion of the gains employees help generate with their ideas with all employees. We recommend organizations *not* start an EDIS with gainsharing.

If the EDIS is a part of a TQ process—and it should be—the organization should be ready to consider gainsharing two to four years into the EDIS evolution as the EDIS moves from stage one to stage two. Gainsharing is equitable, is linked to performance, and is team based.

Gainsharing models are discussed in depth by Edward E. Lawler III in his books *High-Involvement Management* and *Strategic Pay*[6] and by Robert J. Doyle in *Gainsharing and Productivity*.[7]

Prize Systems Start Fast but Fizzle Out Fast Too

Organizations that have used prizes as a primary source of recognition have had fantastic results, both in the quantity and quality of the ideas, *initially*, but such systems soon break down. At first people are excited about a prizes-for-ideas program; they have the opportunity to get a real, tangible prize for an idea they probably tried to sell

---

[6]Edward E. Lawler III, *High-Involvement Management* (San Francisco: Jossey-Bass, 1988); *Strategic Pay* (San Francisco: Jossey-Bass, 1990).

[7]Robert J. Doyle, *Gainsharing and Productivity* (New York: AMACOM, 1983).

to their manager before anyhow. But after the first round or two of prizes, the excitement ends.

Often we've been asked to help organizations that have had prizes-for-ideas programs in place. Typically, we find they are three to six months into the program, the excitement has died down, and their results have dropped dramatically. Either the initial thrill of the prizes has worn off or the prize level has been cut back in some way.

For example, at one company the excitement had been replaced with frustration by the employees, the prize administrator, and the management team. We found:

The employees were frustrated because:

- All of the easy ideas (the plums) had been picked so it was a lot tougher to get a prize.

- The less obvious ideas required teamwork to develop. But no one wanted to work with others on a team because it would mean they would have to share the prize with others.

The prize-program administrator was ready to quit because:

- Keeping track of all the prize winners and of their prize choices had become a full-time job in addition to her existing job responsibilities.

- No one recognized the extent of the workload she had taken on.

- It felt like she was always giving out prizes to others without so much as a thank-you in return.

Management was baffled by it all because:

- They thought their new idea system was going to help them turn the corner in their TQ process. They were looking for improvements in employee morale, customer satisfaction and bottom-line savings.

- They chalked it up as another example of how employee involvement doesn't work.

Although the company wanted us to patch up their prize program and make it work again, our job was really one of damage control. The prize approach had created mistrust between all groups in the company. The employees didn't trust management because they thought management was being too stingy with prizes. The administrator didn't trust the employees because she felt employees were always trying to get more of a prize than they had earned. Management didn't trust employees; they felt employees submitted ideas only for the prizes, not to help improve the company.

When we asked employees what could be done to improve the suggestion system, a common thread to their answers was about prizes. They felt that more prizes and bigger prizes would help them come up with more ideas. The managers, on the other hand, said to scrap the whole program. They said it wasn't worth the headaches and the ill will it had created.

Our solution was to help the company form a true, recognition-based EDIS. We used an approach similar to the one discussed in Chapter 5. The idea-system was primarily created by front-line people. The prize program was dismantled. In the short term, some of the employees felt used and deceived; they boycotted the EDIS. In the long term, almost all of the skeptics became participants and believers—even the management team!

Using prizes for ideas works for only a short time; they don't add value to an EDIS in the long run. Ideas and empowerment thrive on recognition. People will provide their own excitement with a commitment to improve their jobs and the products and services they provide if they:

- know the rules of the "game";
- know their role(s);
- know the company's direction or objective;
- know the score.

Employees need to be empowered to take action and recognized for their actions. Once they are, it's amazing how much they can do and how far they can stretch for both themselves and the organization.

Chapter 5

Starting Up an Employee-Driven Idea System

Starting an Employee-Driven Idea System (EDIS) seems simple at first, but when we look at all of the elements we need to have in place before it's up and running, it can seem overwhelming. In this chapter, the EDIS start-up is broken down into six steps:

Step 1 Establishing the EDIS development team

Step 2 Clarifying the objective of the EDIS

Step 3 Working out the details

Step 4 Implementing the pilot

Step 5 Organizationwide roll out

Step 6 Evaluating and adjusting

Step 1—Establishing the EDIS Development Team

Developing an EDIS is a big task regardless of how simple we try to make it. One person alone can't do it; it requires teamwork. Team members will bring their own rich variety of experiences and ideas to help develop the EDIS; incorporating past experience will result in a more-effective and better-received process.

Who Should Be on the EDIS Development Team?

We have talked to literally hundreds of people who needed guidance in starting up an EDIS. In most cases, the scenario goes something like this:

> I've been assigned the responsibility of developing (or rejuvenating) our suggestion system. Our company is involved in Total Quality Management and this seems like a logical step for us. I have to have the new system in place by the end of the month and I've read some articles about your approach to idea systems. Can you help me? It's important that the system be successful and that the employees are happy with it.

Our first question is always: "Have you asked your employees what they want?"

The answer? Silence.

When we take the time to think about it, it only makes sense that we include front-line employees on the team developing an EDIS. How can we possibly design a system that will make it easy for employees to submit ideas for improvement without first getting their input? That's one reason why most attempts like this fail. We forget to ask the employees what they need.

We recommend that the EDIS development team represent both the breadth and depth of the organization. One person alone cannot develop an EDIS. It is a big project, and it requires the input of employees at various levels in the organization. We've seen organizations make the mistake of assigning the suggestion system to the human resources department. Without any help or input from other departments, they develop the best suggestion system there ever was. The trouble is, it's the best in *their* opinion and *only* their opinion. Ask the employees for whom it was developed what they think and you'll get an entirely different side of the story. Or ask the maintenance department who will be responsible for implementing many of the ideas and they'll tell you why it won't work. A team approach will help you develop a well-rounded system everyone will support.

Breadth

The team should comprise a representative cross section from all areas of the organization. Make sure that the departments to be involved with the day-to-day administration of the EDIS are represented. Some common groups to include are:

- Maintenance
- Manufacturing (or production)
- Finance or accounting
- Communications or marketing
- Engineering
- Manufacturing
- Purchasing
- Human Resources

The team makeup for your organization will depend on your organizational structure, but involvement from all areas of the organization should be sought. The more variety in perspectives, the better the system will be.

Depth

One of the cornerstones of an EDIS is that it gets people involved in making improvements at all levels of the organization. It only makes sense that involvement at all levels begins in the planning stages of the system. Many organizations have made the mistake of not getting input from the front-line employees (for whom the systems are primarily developed) in the development stage. Then, when the system doesn't work, management sits back and wonders why.

Including front-line employees on the development team will help assure that the grand scheme of the system meets the needs of the employees, not the dreams of management. It will also ensure more buy-in to the system once it is established because employees will feel they had a say in its development.

You'll want senior management to be represented on the team as well. Their buy-in is critical for the longevity of the system. They

must be a part of its development or they will not have the commitment necessary to keep it going.

Size of the EDIS Development Team

The EDIS development team should be no larger than 10 people.
Any more than that will make it impossible to act quickly. It will be
difficult to assemble the entire group for meetings or to reach consensus. It's always tough limiting the number of people on a team,
especially when you have more volunteers than openings. If this is
the case for your team, here are some suggestions that might help:

- Start with 10 people who are enthusiastic, excited, and committed
  to the EDIS. Make sure they have a history of following through
  on commitments and that they can stick with the project until it is
  completed. If these people haven't been trained in using continuous improvement (CI) tools, it would be helpful for them to receive
  some training prior to the first meeting. This way, everyone on the
  team will be using a common problem-solving approach and will
  be speaking the same language as they begin to work together.

- Other people can be brought into EDIS development team meetings as needed. If there is someone you feel has a valuable contribution to make, but who doesn't have the time to serve on the
  team full time, you can invite them to join the group when their
  expertise is required.

- When the EDIS is fully developed, the EDIS steering committee
  should form subcommittees to evaluate the progress and make
  improvements in the system. While it makes sense to retain some
  members of the development team on these new committees, it is
  also an opportunity to get others involved in the process.

Table 5.1 provides an example of the EDIS development team
makeup.

Team Ground Rules

As with any team, it's well worth the investment of time to establish
ground rules before plunging into developing the idea system. Use

TABLE 5.1.   The Composition of an EDIS Development Team

Department	Contribution to the EDIS Development Team
Human Resources	Expertise in recognition techniques, motivation, legal issues
Finance	Financial administration, budgeting
Communications/ Marketing	Internal publicity, development of forms
Purchasing, Engineering, Maintenance	Input on how the EDIS should be set up to make it easy to work with their departments.
Front-Line Employees	A realistic view of how the EDIS will be accepted by the employees.

Figure 5.1 as a checklist during your first team meeting to make sure you cover all the important ground rules. The following are some definitions that might help you as you work through the ground rules.

Role of the Team Leader

The role of the team leader is to keep the team focused and make sure that the team has the necessary resources to complete the project.

Role of Team Members

Clarify the roles of the team members. For example:

- Who will take minutes?
- Who will arrange for meeting locations?
- Will everyone on the team be responsible for communicating EDIS development activities to their coworkers and direct superiors?

---

1. **Name the team leader:** _____

2. **Role of team members:**
   Who arranges the meeting location? _____
   Who takes meeting minutes? _____

3. **Meeting ground rules:**
   How often will we meet? _____
   How long will meetings be? _____
   When is the best day and time for meetings? _____
   Will meetings be held if all aren't present? _____

4. **Communication:**
   Will minutes be kept for each meeting? (Sure hope so!) _____
   Will minutes be copied and handed out right at the end of each
   meeting? _____
   Does anyone else get a copy? _____
   Will you schedule your next meeting at the end of this meeting?
   _____

5. **Handling conflict:**
   How long can one person keep the floor? _____
   How long will you spend on one point of disagreement before tabling
   it until the next meeting? (Use the time between meetings to get
   more data!) _____
   Does anyone have veto power over any issue? _____

FIGURE 5.1.   EDIS Development Team Checklist

Meeting Minutes

Meeting minutes document the meeting. There is no need to record every word. Instead, the minutes should serve as an overview of the meeting, describing what actions will result from the meeting and who is responsible, what decisions were made, and what open issues still exist. Finally, the minutes should also indicate when and where the next meeting will be. Figure 5.2 shows an example of a concise format that can be used for team meeting minutes.

Meeting Minutes and Meeting Planner

Date of Meeting:_____ Team Name & No.:_____ Meeting No.:_____

Attended By: _____

Meeting Objectives: 1._____
2._____
3._____
4._____

Decisions Made: 1._____
2._____
3._____
4._____

Action Items:

Item No.	WHAT Will Be Done?	WHO Will Do It?	By WHEN?

Open Issues: 1._____
2._____
3._____

Planning for the Next Meeting:

Who should attend?	Contacted? (Yes or No)	If no, who will contact?	Who should attend?	Contacted? (Yes or No)	If no, who will contact?

Agenda Items: 1._____
2._____
3._____
4._____

Meeting Date: _____   **Start Time:** _____

Where: _____   **End Time:** _____

FIGURE 5.2.   Team Minutes/Agenda Form

Boundaries of Freedom

The boundaries of freedom describe the limits of the team. For example, one boundary may be that the team cannot implement the EDIS without approval from the company president. Another boundary might be that the team must post its minutes on the bulletin board so that everyone in the organization can keep up on what's happening. It's the team's responsibility to get clarification on its boundaries of freedom from the senior management team at the beginning of the project.

Step 2—Clarifying the Objectives of the EDIS

Once the team is formed and *before* everyone jumps into developing the idea system, the team needs to discuss and reach agreement on the basic philosophy of the EDIS. This will help assure that everyone is working toward the same objective.

Start with developing a statement of purpose or a mission statement of the EDIS. The mission statement is a brief, one-sentence description of the purpose of the idea system. Initially, it will serve as the mission for the development team and later will become an effective way to communicate the purpose of the EDIS to the rest of the organization.

Here is an example of a mission statement for an EDIS:

> The Employee Driven Idea System, an integral part of our Continuous Improvement Process, provides a way for individuals to formally submit their ideas for improvement and to participate in the implementation of those ideas as the idea manager/implementor.

We recommend that each organization develop its own EDIS mission statement, but here are some important concepts to include:

- The EDIS is linked with the company's TQ or CI Process
  It's important to clarify that the EDIS is supplemental to the existing TQ process (if there's one in place).

- It focuses on an individual's ideas
  The EDIS is primarily an outlet for individuals to submit ideas.

TABLE 5.2. Basic Guidelines for an EDIS

+ All ideas are equally important.

+ Everyone is eligible to participate in the EDIS.

+ Ideas will be responded to within 5 working days.

+ The goal of the EDIS is for employees to implement their own ideas.

+ The goal of the system is employee involvement and empowerment, not cost-savings.

+ The only bad idea is the one that doesn't get submitted.

- Ideas are formally submitted
  Through the formal submission of ideas, the company can track its progress and the successes of the EDIS.

- Idea initiators (the idea maker) participate in the management (implementation) of their ideas

The EDIS not only provides a way for employees to offer their ideas, it also creates a structure for employees to manage the implementation of their own ideas.

Once the purpose statement has been written, the next thing to do is to develop a set of guidelines for the system.

Table 5.2 shows an example of one team's guidelines for the EDIS.

The EDIS guidelines, together with the purpose statement, will help assure that everyone on the development team has the same understanding of the EDIS. This will help minimize conflict among development-team members down the road.

Step 3—Working out the Details

Now we can start working on the actual development of the EDIS. There are five topics that need to be addressed at this point:

1. Administration
2. Training and communication
3. Recognition and celebration

4. Measurements and improvements

5. Support processes

Depending on the number of people who are working on the EDIS team, you may decide to divide into subcommittees at this point. Each of the five areas can be handled by a two- or three-person subcommittee; the subcommittee's role is to develop the initial plans and bring them back to the full EDIS team for review.

We'll look at each one of these areas in detail.

Administration

Administration refers to the record keeping for the EDIS. It's important that the system be simple for everyone to use; the EDIS administrator, the supervisors (the idea coaches), and the employees (the idea makers, idea managers, and idea installers). The idea form and the idea log are the primary tools for the administrator.

The Idea Form

Figure 5.3 shows an example of an idea form. It may seem too simple at first. But remember, we want the system to encourage people to submit ideas; a complicated form will discourage ideas. The idea form must capture all of the important information about the idea, including:

- who is submitting it;
- the date it is submitted;
- a description of the idea;
- the idea coach's response to the idea;
- two idea-award tickets—one for submitting the idea and one for its implementation.

There are more examples of idea or suggestion forms in Chapter 8. These may help you design one for your organization. Keep in mind, no one likes paperwork, particularly when it appears to add no value, only more work. The more difficult we make it for people to submit ideas, the less ideas we'll get.

HOT IDEA
HANDLE WITH CARE

Name: _____ Department: _____

Here's an idea that I have (please describe it in as much detail as is
necessary for others to understand and appreciate your suggestion):

_____ Date Submitted: _____

Supervisor's Response:

_____ Date Submitted: _____

Initiation Idea Recognition Ticket Idea #: _____	Implementation Idea Recognition Ticket Idea #: _____
Idea Maker: Date Recognized: Idea Coach:	Idea Maker: Idea Manager Idea Installer: Idea Coach: Others: Date Recognized:

FIGURE 5.3.   Idea Form

The Idea Log

We need some type of formal tracking system for the ideas once they
are submitted. A handwritten log, as shown in Figure 5.4, is sufficient
for this purpose. (Although some organizations prefer to keep this
information on a computer, if your organization is small, computer-
ization may be more trouble than it's worth.)

The idea log allows for the tracking of ideas from their original

IDEA LOG

Idea #	Idea Maker	Idea Coach	Date Initiated	Initiation Recognition Date	Implementation Recognition Date	Letter of Deferral

FIGURE 5.4.   Idea Log

submission to implementation. It should serve as a checklist to assure that the employee is given the proper recognition and that the idea is followed through on.

Training and Communication

Training and communication is often forgotten in the excitement to get the EDIS up and running. Organizations sit back and wonder why people don't use it. It's probably because they don't know about it or they don't know how to use it. The EDIS development team will spend most of its time on training and communication issues.

Training

The training that we discuss in this chapter relates specifically to the EDIS. It is assumed that your employees have received some formal training in the basic CI tools. These basic tools will help employees identify and solve problems using the EDIS system. A review of the roles and the tools in an EDIS is provided in Chapters 6 and 7.

EDIS training, especially the training that is done up front, is critical to the successful start-up of the system. Even the best-designed system will fail if people don't know how to use it.

Training should focus on the three key players in the EDIS:

1. The EDIS administrator
2. The idea coaches (supervisors)
3. The idea makers/managers/implementors (employees)

EDIS Administrator Training

The EDIS administrator is responsible for logging and tracking all ideas. Administration can be centralized or contained within each department or division, depending on the size of your organization.

The EDIS administrator will need to know how ideas are to be logged and tracked. A one-on-one training session is sufficient if administration will be centralized. If administration will be handled within each department or division, it's worthwhile to have a training session for all of the administrators together. Administration should be consistent throughout the organization and one common training session will help assure that all administrators are doing the job the same way.

Of course, people come and go, and as administration gets passed from one person to another, there's a risk that slight changes will be made with each new administrator. A flowchart of the administration process will help assure consistency from administrator to administrator.

Idea-Coach Training

As with most quality-related training, companies often make the mistake of forgetting about the supervisor. Take for example one company that had developed an EDIS. They spent months developing the perfect system and another couple of months training employees how to use the system. Unfortunately, the only training the supervisors received was a memo from the EDIS steering committee outlining what they should do when an employee submitted an idea. What a mistake! Although the memo began, "You, the supervisor, are the key to the success of our new Employee Idea System . . . ," it was clear to the supervisors that they were merely the middlemen, the ones who were going to do all of the work and get none of the benefits. Needless to say, the supervisors at that company made sure the idea system didn't work.

The supervisors take the role of idea coaches. They are the pivotal point in the EDIS. During the first year the main function of the idea coaches will be to help employees submit and implement ideas. Once the system is working well and employees grow comfortable submitting ideas, the idea coaches' role changes to that of a true coach, helping employees refine their ideas and to keep the ideas coming. Teaching supervisors about their role in the EDIS is the most important and valuable training you will do. In fact, it's so important that if you could only train one group of people, it should be this group. The role they will play cannot be learned from a memo. If their training needs are ignored or if they are not properly trained, the idea system fails. With the supervisors squarely behind it and well prepared for their new role, EDIS will be a success.

What training do supervisors need? Training should include:

1. The philosophy of the EDIS
2. Supervisors' role and the roles others play in the EDIS
3. EDIS administration
4. Using internal processes to get ideas implemented

They must be proficient in all four areas before the companywide roll out of the EDIS. It may seem like a lot, but a minimum of eight hours should be spent on supervisor training. Four two-hour sessions spread over two to four weeks will break the training into manageable chunks and help avoid information overload. Figure 5.5 shows a recommended course schedule for training supervisors in the EDIS.

(8 hours)

Day 1 (2 hours)—Tapping the Kaizen Mine
1.1 The difference between a traditional suggestion system and an EDIS
1.2 Why an EDIS works
1.3 The value of Kaizen ideas
1.4 How an EDIS works

Day 2 (2 hours)—Roles and Responsibilities
2.1 The supervisor's role as idea coach
2.2 The role of the EDIS Steering Committee
2.3 The role of the employees

Day 3 (2 hours)—EDIS Mechanics
3.1 What happens when an employee submits an idea
3.2 Idea administration for supervisors
3.3 Measures of participation and supervisor accountability

Day 4 (2 hours)—Working the System
4.1 Using internal systems:
　　a. Petty cash
　　b. Maintenance work orders
　　c. Purchasing
4.2 Communicating the EDIS message to employees
4.3 EDIS roll out plans

FIGURE 5.5. Recommended EDIS Training for Supervisors

(2 hours)

1. The value of Kaizen ideas
2. How an EDIS works to tap the Kaizen Mine
3. How an EDIS differs from a traditional suggestion system
4. Roles and responsibilities in the EDIS:
   Supervisors
   Employees
   EDIS Steering Committee
5. How to submit an idea and what happens to it from there

FIGURE 5.6. Recommended EDIS Training for Employees

Idea Maker/Manager/Installer Training

If the supervisors are well trained, they should be able to train their employees in EDIS. However, they should not be the ones to introduce employees to the new system. The introduction should be done by top management and/or the EDIS steering committee.

It is certainly important that employees understand how the idea system works if they are going to be expected to use it. Employee training can be an abbreviated (two-hour) version of the supervisor training covering some similar topics. Most of the session should detail how to submit an idea and how the recognition-system works. Employee-training topics should include:

1. The philosophy of the EDIS
2. The roles of the people involved in the EDIS
3. How to submit and implement ideas
4. The recognition/reward system

Figure 5.6 shows a sample training outline.

If your organization is large, you should train groups of 15 to 20 employees at a time. The small-group approach will encourage people to participate and ask questions.

Communication

Once the training is complete, it's important for people to be constantly reminded of the EDIS. A communication system must be established to keep people posted on the progress of the EDIS and to publicize the implementation of ideas. EDIS communication can be done within departments or divisions, companywide or both depending on the size of the organization. A dedicated EDIS communication center or bulletin board will help. You'll want to divide the bulletin board to highlight a variety of information such as EDIS statistics, the EDIS mission, guidelines and procedures, and examples of ideas that have been implemented. The following are some ideas for your bulletin board.

Idea Scorecard

The scorecard (Figure 5.7) keeps track of how many ideas each employee has submitted and implemented. On this scorecard, the top half of each block for each idea indicates when an idea has been submitted. The bottom half is filled in when the idea is implemented. You can also color code the blocks to make the scorecard easier to read.

IDEA SCORECARD
1st Quarter

Number of Ideas Submitted

Employee	1	2	3	4	5	6	7	8	9	10
Ricky Lauser	☆	☆	☆							
Alvin Rhoade	☆	☆	☆	☆	☆	☆	☆	☆	☆	☆
Dick Quartno	☆									
Chuck Cardigan	☆	☆	☆	☆	☆	☆	☆			
Jon Rutlange	☆	☆								
Cris Leganos	☆	☆	☆	☆	☆	☆	☆			
Carol Michaels	☆	☆	☆	☆	☆					
Jay Elliott	☆	☆	☆	☆						
Debbie Briggs	☆	☆	☆	☆	☆					
Gerry Spriter	☆	☆	☆	☆						

FIGURE 5.7. Idea Scorecard

Idea Trend Chart

The idea trend chart tracks the number of ideas submitted and implemented on a weekly (or monthly) basis. At the end of each week (or month), the number of ideas submitted that week is posted on the chart. This will give everyone a quick indication of whether the number of ideas are going up or down on a weekly basis. You can also track the number of ideas implemented on the same chart. Figure 5.8 shows an idea trend chart.

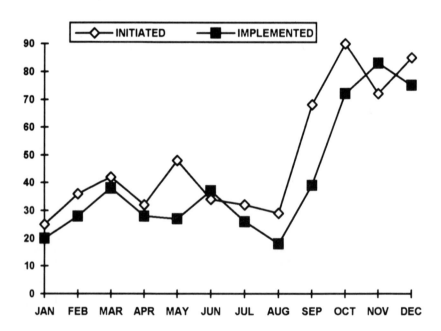

FIGURE 5.8.   Idea Trend Chart

Participation Thermometer

The participation thermometer displays the current participation rate or the number of employees who have submitted at least one idea within the given time period. As the participation rate increases, the thermometer is raised accordingly. Figure 5.9 provides an example of a participation thermometer.

Idea Highlights

On a weekly basis you should post a few of the ideas submitted and implemented during the previous week. This will give the idea makers recognition for their participation and publicize the success of the EDIS. You do run the risk of some people feeling left out because you didn't choose to post their ideas. Random selection (perhaps by drawing) of the ideas to be posted will help guard against claims of favoritism.

FIGURE 5.9. Participation Thermometer

Quarterly-Award Winners

If you give quarterly awards for ideas, you'll want to feature those ideas and the idea makers on the bulletin board as well. An inexpensive Polaroid camera will provide you with pictures of the idea makers.

Other Forms of Communication

Information on the EDIS should be included in any communication you have with employees such as newsletters, announcements, paycheck stuffers, or regular meetings. Companies that have sent information about the EDIS to employees' homes have found that it's an excellent way to promote the idea system. Often, an employee's family will encourage him or her to participate. At one company, an employee continuously griped to his wife about a problem he had at work. When his wife learned about the EDIS, she suggested he submit his idea for improvement on an EDIS form to his supervisor. Her urging caused the employee to take the first step and he submitted and eventually implemented a top-notch idea.

Recognition and Celebration

In Chapter 4 we discussed the importance of recognition over rewards and the difference between the two. Reward is defined as something of financial value such as a cash payout, merchandise, or a travel certificate commensurate with the financial impact of the idea. A reward system such as this introduces complexity and competition into the EDIS. Instead, the EDIS should be simple to administer and foster teamwork throughout the organization. EDIS philosophy says that the true reward of getting an idea implemented is that a job has been made simpler, quality has improved, or customer satisfaction (internal or external) has increased. Continually improving processes is part of everyone's job; it's not something above and beyond the call of duty. Ultimately everyone in the organization will reap the benefits of the EDIS by being part of an organization that increases its competitive position as a result of its continual improvement.

Recognition provides a formal process of acknowledgment for an employee's involvement in the EDIS. It provides a way to reinforce positive behavior and thank employees for their involvement. Regular recognition will keep employees involved and enthusiastic about the EDIS.

Levels of Recognition

Recognition can occur on many levels. Individual recognition is most common in an EDIS. There are many opportunities for individual recognition including:

- When the idea is submitted
- When the idea is implemented
- When a certain number of ideas have been submitted by an individual
- At the end of a time period if a certain number of ideas have been submitted by an individual
- For an outstanding idea as judged by peers (e.g., top-10 ideas of the quarter)
- For helping an idea maker with an idea

Recognizing the idea maker for submitting an idea is obvious, but don't forget about those people behind the scenes such as the idea coaches, the idea managers, and the idea installers who help put the ideas into action. Take, for example, people in the maintenance department. While most of the ideas will come from people on the front line, employees in the maintenance department will often be involved in the idea's implementation. If two maintenance employees help implement the idea, they should both receive recognition for their efforts. And don't forget about the people in purchasing and engineering or the EDIS administrator, either. While the idea maker sparked the idea, a whole team is often needed to put it into action.

Table 5.3 provides an example of how the recognition system can work.

Keeping track of who assisted with an idea can be a nightmare. The person who has the best knowledge of everyone's involvement is the idea manager. The idea manager should be responsible for

TABLE 5.3.   EDIS Recognition System Matrix

Who Should be Recognized

What to recognize for?	Idea Maker	Idea Manager	Idea Installer	Idea Coach
Submitting an idea	$1			
The implementation of the idea	$1	$1	$1	$1
Best Idea of the Quarter	Dinner or merchandise certificate.			Personal note from the leader of the organization.
Achieving a personal milestone for number of ideas	Opportunity to visit a customer.	Opportunity to attend a seminar.	Opportunity to attend a trade show.	Personal note from the leader of the organization.

*The recognition strategy in this matrix is simply an example. For more comprehensive ideas on recognition, see Chapter 4 and Chapter 8.

recognition of the others in the idea support team who have helped with the idea. Whether you give out coupons, dollar bills, or lottery tickets, the idea manager should have easy access to these tokens for distribution to the rest of the team.

In addition to individual recognition, you can also recognize departments, divisions, or the entire organization for their participation. You just need to be careful not to turn it into a competition between groups. For example, a contest between departments for the highest percent participation during the quarter means that one department will win and all others will lose. Even if the winning department has 95 percent participation and all others have 90 percent participation (which, by the way, is darned good all around!), there's still only one winner and a lot of losers. Setting up a competition such as this will ultimately undermine teamwork. A better approach is to establish a milestone for everyone to work toward. If all groups achieve the milestone, they will all have earned the special recognition; everyone can be a winner.

Companywide celebrations for achieving certain milestones provide another outlet for recognition. Milestones worthy of celebration include:

- Achieving 75 percent participation in the EDIS (75 percent of the employees have submitted at least one idea)
- Receiving the one-thousandth idea
- Achieving an 80 percent implementation rate
- Reducing turnaround time for idea approval to two days
- The average number of ideas per employee per year exceeds five

Types of Recognition and Celebration

Recognition in its simplest form is a pat on the back and thanks for a job well done. Many managers discount the power of this common courtesy. They reason that employees are getting paid to do their job, and that should be sufficient motivation. Or that giving someone a pat on the back without handing out a monetary bonus is an insult. Both of these notions are ridiculous. Everyone needs to know they are doing the right things right. Otherwise, how do they know they should continue doing them?

A formal recognition system will provide structure and assure that everyone is recognized for their contribution. In the hustle and bustle of daily activities, it's easy to forget about giving someone a pat on the back. It's often put off for later, but later never comes. In addition, because everyone has their own unique style, there can be a great inconsistency in the way the pat on the back comes about; for one manager it may mean a formal celebration with all employees present, while for another it may mean a casual word of thanks while passing in the hallway. A formal recognition system assures consistency.

Most companies that have had long-term success with an EDIS use surprisingly small tokens of appreciation such as a dollar bill, a

$1 lottery ticket, or a $1 coupon that can be saved for larger gifts or gift certificates to local stores or attractions such as movies or sporting events. You might be thinking, "Big deal," just as we did when we first heard about $1 tokens. However, employees respond to it favorably because the recognition is immediate. A hidden benefit is that $1 tokens of appreciation won't break the bank and we won't be tempted to withhold the appreciation to save money. Many companies reduce the value of awards as cost-cutting measures during tough times. It's a lot easier to justify $1 awards than it is to justify $10 or $25 awards when expenses must be cut.

Recognition for Making and Implementing Ideas

An EDIS focuses on getting a lot of ideas, so it's important to give recognition for each idea submitted whether or not it will be implemented. Employees will soon get the message that their involvement is valued. Of course you should also provide recognition when the idea is implemented. Some organizations give the same award when the idea is submitted and when it is implemented. For example, $1 when the idea is submitted and another $1 when the idea is implemented. Others give a bigger award for implementation. For example, one company gives $1 when the idea is submitted and $2 when an idea is implemented.

Personal Milestones

Recognition for achieving milestones, such as when employees submit their tenth idea within a quarter, should be more substantial than the award for submitting one idea, but it need not be excessive. For example, if you give out $1 coupons for submitting an idea, you may award five bonus coupons when the milestone is achieved. You might also add the employee's name to a plaque honoring those who have reached this milestone.

Quarterly Awards

Quarterly awards for the top-five ideas implemented may seem counterproductive to teamwork but, if handled the right way, it can be an important source of peer recognition. Rather than having the judges of the top idea of the quarter be management personnel, the judging committee should be a representative cross section of the organization, a peer-recognition committee. Eight to ten people is a good size for this committee. One way of selecting committee members is to have the people who won the awards in the previous quarter rotate on to the committee and have the five people who have been on the committee the longest rotate off.

Using boundaries of freedom from the EDIS steering committee, the peer-recognition committee could be responsible for developing the criteria for judging the awards. It should be documented so that as people rotate through the committee, there is some consistency in the way ideas are selected. With membership of the committee constantly changing, fresh perspectives and new ways of identifying the top ideas of the quarter will be found, so there should be some flexibility in the criteria. In developing the criteria, remind the committee that the "best" ideas aren't necessarily the ones that yield the biggest cost savings; they may be the ideas that made a significant safety or housekeeping improvement. Figure 5.10 is an example of a rating form used for judging ideas.

Idea Number: _____

Submitted by: _____

Criteria	Points (0 to 10)	Weight	Score (Points x Weight)
Creativity/Originality		10	
Usage of CI Tools		10	
Impact on Others		10	
Severity of the Situation		10	
Teamwork/Coordination		7	
Cost to Implement		5	

Total Points

FIGURE 5.10.   Quarterly Recognition Judging Form

Winners of the quarterly awards for the top ideas deserve special recognition. One company gives each recipient a framed certificate of achievement and has the employee's name added to the "Top Idea" plaque hung in the main lobby. In addition, the employee is invited to attend the annual dinner honoring "Top Idea" recipients and their spouses.

Recognizing Idea Coaches, Managers, and Installers

Implementation of any idea requires teamwork. The idea coach helps the idea maker formulate the idea and make it work. The idea manager (who may or may not be the same as the idea maker) coordinates the installation of the idea. The idea installers are the ones who make the idea a reality by implementing it. It's important that these folks receive recognition for their contribution to the idea.

The best person to judge each party's contribution to the implementation is the idea maker. He or she knows what it took to implement the idea and needs a way to thank the rest of the team. It makes sense, then, that the idea maker be the one responsible for recognition of the rest of the team. Your development team must include a process for handling this level of recognition. One suggestion is to have the idea maker award the recognition tokens directly to the others who were instrumental in the implementation of the idea. The process may require that he or she give their names to the idea coach. The idea coach, in turn, would give him the recognition tokens to give to those who assisted him and he would present them to the deserving parties. The recognition token should be just that—a token, nothing of real financial value. For example, if your recognition for the idea maker is a $1 coupon, then you could give the same form of recognition to the idea coach, idea manager, and idea installers.

Publicize your EDIS Successes

Anytime you have a chance to publicize the success of your idea system, the idea makers, or the idea coaches, managers, and installers, grab the opportunity. Whether it's in a departmental award ceremony, the company picnic, or the local newspaper, publicity for the people who are making the EDIS work brings more energy to the EDIS.

Measurements and Improvement

It's a mistake to put an EDIS in place and assume that because it looks good on paper, everything is going great. You need to measure the results of the system and compare them with your expectations so you can identify opportunities for improvement.

Measurements

Some common EDIS measures are:

- Number of ideas per eligible employee per year
- Percent participation (number of employees who have submitted at least one idea during the year)
- Implementation turnaround time
- Percent of ideas implemented
- Percent of ideas submitted by each department or division
- Percent of ideas submitted by employee category.

While statistics such as these are important, it's dangerous to only focus on the numbers and ignore how employees *feel* about the EDIS. It's a good idea to regularly survey your organization to find out what they think of the EDIS and what ideas they have to make it better (just in case they haven't formally submitted them through the EDIS). Figure 5.11 is an example of an employee survey to determine satisfaction with the EDIS.

Measuring Economic Impact

We don't recommend spending a lot of time figuring out how much money the ideas have saved the company, especially in the early stages of an EDIS when the objective is to get a lot of ideas. Savings for many ideas will be tough to measure. It's nearly impossible to

Fellow Associate:

Please take a few minutes to complete this survey on our Employee Idea System. Your input and ideas will be valuable as we begin our annual review and improvement of our EDIS.

Thank you!

1. How many ideas have you submitted this year? _____

2. How many of your ideas have been installed? _____

For the following questions, please answer as follows:
1 = Strongly Agree   **3 = Disagree**
2 = Agree   **4 = Strongly Disagree**
N/A = Does not apply

3. The Idea System provides an excellent way for
me to express my ideas and get them acted upon.   1   2   3   4   **N/A**

4. It is critical to the success of this company that
we have a system to capture and act on all   1   2   3   4   **N/A**
employees' ideas.

5. My supervisor is supportive of the ideas I
present to him/her.   1   2   3   4   **N/A**

6. My supervisor encourages us to constantly
think of new and better ways to do our job.   1   2   3   4   **N/A**

7. I am very satisfied with our Idea System.   1   2   3   4   **N/A**

Please put any comments or suggestions you have on the back of this survey.

FIGURE 5.11. Employee Survey to Determine Satisfaction with EDIS

measure the value of intangible ideas such as a safety improvement. Rather than spend nonvalue-adding time trying to calculate a dollar value for an intangible idea, assign an arbitrary dollar value, such as $100, to those ideas. This amount can be added to the amount for tangible ideas to get a rough estimate of the overall savings due to the EDIS.

Don't Misuse Measures

You must be careful not to misuse any data you collect on the EDIS. If you use it as a stick against departments or people, thinking it will motivate them to do better, you're wrong. The real purpose of measurements should be to identify pockets of excellence to share and build on and opportunities for improvement.

Improvement

An EDIS should be dynamic; it should not be allowed to stagnate. As it matures and you identify opportunities for improvement, develop plans to make the improvements happen. Some organizations formally assess the EDIS once a year and update it on a regular basis. Others make changes as necessary rather than at a set time interval.

It's important that everyone understand that there will be changes made to the system from time to time so people aren't surprised by the improvements.

More information on improvements will be discussed later in this chapter when we review step 6—evaluating and adjusting.

Support Processes

Since one of the goals of the EDIS is to turn the idea makers into the idea managers and implementors, people will need to know how to work the system to get things done. We certainly don't want people working *around* the system, yet often the systems or support processes themselves encourage this because they are so complicated and difficult to use. It's surprising how few people really know how processes such as petty cash, work orders, and purchasing actually work, yet these processes supposedly exist to serve the organization. These will probably be the first items to look at because they will be the most frequently used during the first couple of years of the EDIS.

Often, the existing processes complicate the idea-implementation process. These processes will need to be streamlined and simplified. You'll probably be surprised at the nonvalue-adding steps that bog down your processes and create headaches for everyone involved.

For example, one company had a policy that petty cash distribution required the signature of both the accounting manager and the purchasing director. This requirement was instituted five years earlier when the company was trying to stop people from purchasing anything without going through the purchasing department. The difficult approval process included an interrogation of anyone needing petty cash. When the EDIS was instituted, the company streamlined the petty-cash process, removing the purchasing department from the loop. Instead, guidelines were established and communicated to everyone in the organization regarding the use of petty cash for purchasing supplies. A dollar limit was established for purchases with petty-cash money, and employees were encouraged to discuss petty-cash purchases with the purchasing department in advance. While there was still a chance that the process would be abused, the time savings by streamlining the process made it well worth the risk.

The best way to document your support processes so everyone can understand how to use them is by using a flowchart. Figure 5.12 shows the flowchart for the revised petty-cash process for the example we just reviewed.

Part of the training for idea coaches, idea makers, idea managers, and idea implementors should cover use of these support processes. It is also helpful to provide each department with a notebook of the documented process. This way, when someone is making or implementing an idea, the reference will be close at hand. Table 5.4 lists the support processes to include in the documentation.

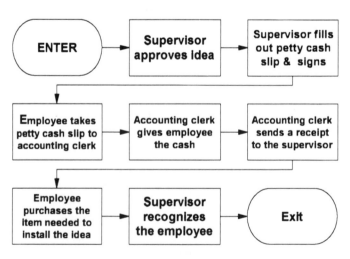

FIGURE 5.12.   Flowchart for the Petty-Cash Process

TABLE 5.4. EDIS Support-Process Documentation

✦ How to request petty cash

✦ How to complete maintenance work orders

✦ How to work with the purchasing department

✦ How to request capital projects

✦ How to get help from the engineering department

✦ How to get help from the maintenance department

✦ How to get help from other departments

Step 4—Implementing the Pilot

A lot of work has taken place so far and we still haven't started the EDIS. As usual, however, the time spent up front in the planning stage will more than pay for itself in the implementation stage.

An EDIS will be a new process to the organization; therefore, there will be plenty of opportunities for improvement identified early on. For this reason, if your organization is large, start by conducting a pilot in a small area of the organization. The pilot will allow you to test the EDIS and make improvements before the EDIS goes companywide.

Planning for the Pilot

With the details of the EDIS worked out, we're ready to begin the pilot. There are several things to consider, such as:

- What group will participate in the pilot?
- What is the timeframe for the pilot?
- How will we tell the rest of the organization about the pilot?
- How will we evaluate the pilot?

What Group Will Participate in the Pilot?

We want the pilot to be a success, but we also want it to be a realistic simulation of the EDIS, so the group you select for the pilot is important. Keep in mind that each group, department or division within an organization has its own personality. Some are cooperative and willing to try new things while others have a wait-and-see attitude. For the pilot to succeed, we obviously need a group that will give the EDIS a fair chance of succeeding and provide feedback on how to improve the idea system before it is introduced. We'll need to train the pilot before it is started.

What Is the Timeframe for the Pilot?

A two- to three-month trial is a good timeframe for the EDIS pilot. One month is too short; the newness of the EDIS will affect people's reaction to it and we'll get some unrealistic assessments of the pilot. For example, there will be more participation during the first month the EDIS is introduced. Allowing another month or two for the process to settle in will assure we get an accurate picture of the areas that need improvement before the organizationwide roll out.

How Will the Rest of the Organization Be Told About the Pilot?

The EDIS pilot should not be a mystery to the rest of the organization. They should be informed about the purpose of the EDIS and know why a pilot is being conducted before the organizationwide roll out. Keep people updated by including announcements on the bulletin board or through articles in the company newsletter. This will help introduce the concept of the EDIS to the organization so that when it does go organizationwide, it won't be a surprise, but rather, something people are anxiously waiting for. If the publicity on the pilot is handled well, there will be tremendous excitement about the new idea system before it even gets off the ground.

How Will the Pilot Be Evaluated?

The purpose of the pilot is to test the EDIS in a small part of the organization and make improvements based on the feedback of the pilot participants. Because the pilot affects only a small number of people, improvements to the system can be made and evaluated as soon as they are identified. However, some formal way to evaluate the effectiveness of the EDIS in the pilot situation is needed. As we discussed in step 3—working out the details—measurements are important. In the pilot you'll want to measure:

- Ideas per week
- Participation rate
- Average ideas per employee
- Implementation turnaround time

These should provide a good idea of what to expect when the EDIS goes organizationwide. If the numbers do not meet expectations, find out why. The best place to get that information is from the employees themselves. Rather than using a survey to get this information from the pilot groups, conduct focus groups.

Focus groups are an excellent way to find out how people feel about the EDIS pilot. A good size for a focus group is five or six pilot participants with a focus-group leader. Include idea makers, idea coaches, idea managers, and implementors in the groups. The focus-group leader (preferably a neutral person from outside the EDIS development team) walks the group through a series of questions about the EDIS pilot. The group setting will encourage people to speak freely and develop creative solutions to problems they've found with the system. Conducting two or three different focus groups will provide valuable information for adjusting the EDIS prior to taking it organizationwide.

Step 5—Organizationwide Roll Out

Once the EDIS is fully developed on paper and tested through a pilot, it is ready for roll out. It may be tempting to introduce the EDIS with fanfare and hoopla, but this is not the best approach. Employees can see through it and will tend to sit back and take a wait-and-see attitude. (After all, they've probably seen plenty of programs come in with gusto only to die a quick death in actual implementation.)

Save the celebration for later when successes to commemorate are real. For now, training should be focused on idea makers, managers, coaches, and installers. The training will provide the tools everyone needs to make the system a success.

Use the information gained during the pilot to fuel the company-wide roll out. Publicize the successes of the pilot, citing specific examples of ideas that were made and implemented. Share the data collected on the pilot such as participation and implementation statistics, as well as positive feedback from the focus groups. Build this good news into the training. Success fuels more success and if people know that the system has worked in one part of the organization, they will be more likely to believe it will work in their area.

Step 6—Evaluating and Adjusting

Measuring the Success of the EDIS—Stage 1 Measures

As we discussed earlier in this chapter, in the spirit of continuous improvement, always look for ways to make the EDIS better, regardless of how good the initial design is. Only by measuring the results of the EDIS against expectations or goals can we determine what needs to be improved. Goals for the first year should be established before the EDIS is rolled out to the organization. Everyone should be made aware of them during the training so they can be used as a scorecard throughout the year. It is particularly helpful to compare your statistics with those of other organizations. Table 5.5 compares statistics for the United States and Japan and recommends realistic goals for the first year of your EDIS. While we've already discussed some of the most common statistics earlier in this chapter, we'll review them in more detail now. Table 5.6 shows all the formulas for the calculations of these statistics.

Ideas Per Eligible Employee

Since we recommend that everyone in the organization be eligible, this measurement is more appropriately called "ideas per employee." It will help you track the quantity of ideas you are receiving. Because it

TABLE 5.5.   EDIS Statistics: U.S., Japan, and First-Year Goals

MEASURE	JAPAN	U.S.	1st Year GOALS
Ideas per Eligible Employee	32	0.17	8
Participation Rate	65%	10%	50%*
Average Turnaround Time	N/A	N/A	1 Week
Implementation Rate	87%	33%	75%
Financial Return Per Adoption	$129	$7,102	N/A
Financial Return Per Employee	$3,612	$398	N/A

*Although this may seem high, the first year is when you'll get the most ideas because of the newness of the system.

Source for US and Japan statistics: Michael Verespej, "Suggestion Systems Gain New Luster," *Industry Week*, November 16, 1992, p. 18.

is standardized, use it to compare results from quarter to quarter, year to year, or to compare your organization to another regardless of differences in size. In Japan, employees submit an average of 32 suggestions per year versus U.S. employees who submit an average of 0.17 suggestions per year.

Participation Rate

This statistic is what percent of the work force has submitted at least one idea. It will help assess what portion of the work force is participating in the EDIS. Ideally it would be 100 percent, but 50 percent

TABLE 5.6.   Calculations for EDIS Statistics

MEASURE	CALCULATION
Ideas per Eligible Employee	Number of ideas divided by the number of eligible employees
Participation Rate	Number of employees who have submitted at least one idea divided by the total number of eligible employees times 100%
Average Turnaround Time	Total of the time it took to turnaround all ideas divided by the number of ideas
Implementation Rate	Number of ideas implemented divided by the total number of ideas submitted times 100%
Financial Return Per Adoption	Total of the financial savings for all ideas divided by the number of ideas
Financial Return Per Employee	Total of the financial savings for all ideas divided by the number of eligible employees

participation in the first year would be a more realistic objective. Companies with successful systems in place find that the participation rate drops off after the first year but holds steady in subsequent years. In Japan, over 65 percent of the employees participate in an EDIS versus 15 percent participation in a traditional U.S. suggestion system.

Turnaround Time

One of the major improvements an EDIS offers to a traditional suggestion system is speed of implementation. With an EDIS, implementation is measured in days or sometimes even hours compared with months for most traditional suggestion systems. One reason for this is that the ideas are smaller, requiring less analysis and planning to implement. One week would be a good target for the first year of the EDIS. Benchmark U.S. companies boast a 72-hour turnaround time.

Implementation Rate

Objectives for the first year should include a target for the percent of ideas implemented. Obviously, the higher the better since employees will get discouraged if they keep submitting ideas that are rejected and not implemented. Nearly 9 out of every 10 ideas (87 percent) submitted in Japan are implemented compared with 33 percent (or 1 out of every 3) ideas in the United States. That means that in the United States, workers have a two in three chance of their idea being rejected. (It's no wonder there are so few ideas submitted in the United States!)

Measuring the Success of the EDIS— Stage 2 and 3 Measures

As your idea system evolves into stage two or three, look at some other statistics that measure the value-adding impact of ideas. This will help you identify what training is needed to help people improve the "quality" of their ideas. However, look at these measures only when the participation rate is at an acceptable level. Focusing on them prematurely will send the wrong message to the organization.

Savings Per Idea

Some ideas will have tangible savings but many will not. We recommend calculating the savings by adding the tangible savings plus a constant value (e.g., $100) per idea with an intangible saving. Dividing the savings by the number of ideas gives the savings per idea. The net savings per idea submitted alone doesn't tell us much. It does help compare an EDIS system from year to year and compare it to other companies' systems. While we would like the number to go up each year, we don't want that to happen at the expense of a drop off in the participation rate. If employees feel that the focus of the EDIS has shifted from employee participation to bottom-line savings, they'll stop submitting those ideas that yield little or no tangible savings to the company. In Japan, the savings-per-idea average was $129 compared with $7,102 per idea in the United States. But, keep in mind, U.S. employees submit an average of 0.17 ideas per person per year versus 32 ideas per person in Japan. The net savings per employee is much higher in Japan even though the net savings per suggestion is lower.

Savings Per Employee

By dividing the savings by the number of employees, we can calculate the average savings per employee. The annual savings on a per-employee basis is nearly 10 times higher in Japan ($3,612 compared with $398) than the U.S. rate. This calculation is more meaningful than the savings per idea.

Internal Comparisons

There are also some statistics that can be used for internal comparisons between departments or divisions. Remember, however, don't create internal competition; after all, all departments are on the same team. Depending on the organizational structure, we can calculate all of the statistics on a departmental or job-function basis. Remember, the data shouldn't be used as a weapon, but rather to identify if any one department is doing better than the others. If you find this to be true, study what the department is doing right and have them help other departments or groups.

Frequency of Measurement

Evaluation should be done on a regular basis such as quarterly, semi-annually, or annually. Evaluation dates should be planned in advance and everyone should know when they are. Once a couple of evaluation periods are complete it will be much easier to establish future goals.

Adjusting

If the EDIS isn't meeting objectives and expectations, it's time to take a hard look at it and identify where the problem is. Table 5.7 shows some of the most common problems encountered during the first year of an EDIS and some possible causes. Remember, the best source for improvement ideas are the employees themselves.

If the EDIS is meeting objectives, set your sights higher. For example, if the goal was 60 percent participation the first year and 60 percent was achieved, rather than shooting for the same thing next year raise expectations. It's great that 60 percent of the people chose

TABLE 5.7.   Potential Problems with an EDIS During the First Year

Effect	Possible Cause
Employees are not submitting many ideas	• They are suspicious that the EDIS will be another "program of the month" • Supervisors aren't working with employees to help them submit ideas • Ineffective training • Employees are getting mixed messages about the EDIS
Supervisors don't seem to be buying into the EDIS	• The system was made more complicated than necessary • Ineffective training • Lack of buy-in to the Continuous Improvement Process
Management is not supporting the EDIS	• Lack of commitment to the EDIS • Lack of understanding of the EDIS • Goals and objectives that conflict with the EDIS

Step 1 - Establishing the EDIS Development Team

❒   The team represents both the breadth and depth of the organization.
❒   Team Ground Rules have been set.

Step 2 - Clarifying the Objective of the EDIS

❒   We have a Mission Statement for the EDIS and it is supported by the management of our organization.

Step 3 - Working out the Details

❒   Procedures for administering the EDIS have been established and communicated to the appropriate people.
❒   Training for supervisors has been conducted.
❒   Employees have been trained in how to use the EDIS.
❒   We have established a way to assure regular communication on the EDIS.
❒   A recognition system that incorporates recognition of idea makers, managers, installers, and coaches has been designed and the appropriate personnel have been trained in how to use it.
❒   We have decided on what statistics we will use to measure the EDIS and have established a process to assure accurate collection of this information.
❒   There is a feedback loop in place to enable employees to make suggestions to improve the EDIS.
❒   Support processes have been documented to make it easier for others to use them. If they seemed too difficult, they were modified.

FIGURE 5.13.   Checklist for Developing an EDIS

to submit at least one idea, but what about the other 40 percent? Two out of every five people did not participate. Why not? Or let's say the goal was to have 75 percent of all ideas implemented within one week of being submitted. Perhaps 90 percent of all ideas were implemented within one week. Maybe next year the goal should be changed from one week to three days. Remember, there is always room for improvement.

Step 4 - Implementing the Pilot

❏ A representative area has been selected to pilot the EDIS.
❏ The rest of the organization has been informed of the pilot.
❏ We have established a process to determine the effectiveness of the pilot, including measures and employee feedback.

Step 5 - Organizationwide Rollout

❏ We have made improvements in the EDIS based on feedback from the pilot.
❏ We have completed all initial employee and supervisor EDIS training.

Step 6 - Evaluating and Adjusting

❏ We regularly measure key factors of the EDIS and track them over time.
❏ We have established goals for the first year of the EDIS.
❏ We have an annual review process established to audit the EDIS and identify opportunities for improvement.

FIGURE 5.13. (Continued)

Conclusion

In this chapter we've tried to provide a step-by-step guide to developing and implementing an EDIS. Figure 5.13 can be used as a checklist by your development team to make sure you haven't missed anything along the way.

Chapter 6

Roles and Responsibilities in an Employee-Driven Idea System

To get the most from an Employee-Driven Idea System (EDIS), all employees must be involved. There's no room for those who don't want to be involved. Long term, we must harness the creativity and ideas of everyone in the organization. There is no other way to achieve the continuous improvement (CI) that we'll need in the future for the survival and growth or our organization.

While employees must be involved in coming up with new ideas for improvement, it doesn't stop there. Employees also have roles in refining, managing, implementing, and even following up on their ideas. But management, supervisors, and support groups play important roles in an EDIS as well. In this chapter we'll discuss the various roles in an EDIS: the role of the employees, their supervisors, management, the idea-system steering committee, and the union (where applicable). All of these roles differ, yet there are overlaps between the groups. (See Figure 6.1 for an EDIS organization chart.) And roles are not stagnant; they will evolve as the organization's total quality (TQ) process evolves. Since management and supervi-

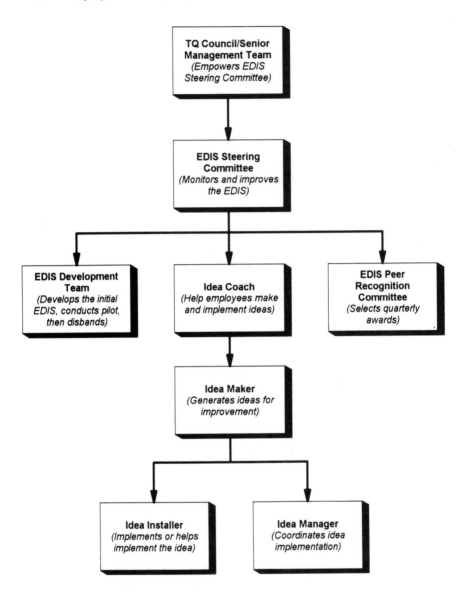

FIGURE 6.1. EDIS Organization Chart

sors play the most critical roles in the success of an EDIS, we'll start with them.

Role of Management

Lead, follow, or get out of the way. This has become a popular phrase in TQ, and applies to everyone in the organization but management. Management's role is to lead the organization and the TQ process. Members of the management team who don't want the responsibility or who are going to get in the way of CI efforts will kill the process. An EDIS, as part of a CI effort requires management leadership and commitment as well.

Leading an EDIS includes:

- Creating the environment
- Developing, administering, and auditing the system

Creating the Environment

Management creates the environment for an EDIS by:

- providing training for all employees, for supervisors, and even for themselves;
- communicating information about the EDIS;
- establishing a recognition system where they (top management) are personally involved;
- celebrating the successes.

Training

Management doesn't have to do the training but they do have to make sure it happens. They can empower others to develop and provide training on the details of the EDIS, such as how to submit and implement ideas and how supervisors can coach employees. In Chapter 5 we discussed in greater detail the training your organization will need to provide. Management must support the training effort by providing the resources (time, money, people) and by taking an active role as a participant in the training.

Communication

The EDIS provides abundant opportunities for management to communicate with the rest of the organization. It must assure everyone in the organization is kept up to date on the status (and the evolution) of the idea system. This communication should include discussing trends in the number of ideas, participation levels, and future plans, always reinforcing its support and commitment to the EDIS. This should be done in regular employee meetings, through newsletters, and in one-on-one meetings. Constant reminders about the EDIS will reinforce the integral role the EDIS plays in the organization.

Recognition

Employee ideas thrive on recognition. Management must understand this and assure that comprehensive recognition is built into the EDIS. (See Chapter 4.) As with training, management needn't be the one to develop the recognition system, but it must use it.

Top management's personal involvement in recognizing employees is most important. This cannot be delegated or done through internal mail or voice mail. It must be face to face. Personal involvement is more than just being briefed on highly successful ideas and lauding them in a company newsletter, at an organizationwide meeting, or in an awards ceremony. While these are part of the recognition strategy, personal involvement means spending time out in the organization with the employees and personally acknowledging them for their ideas.

This may seem to be an impossible task for busy executives in large organizations and organizations with multiple sites. Day-to-day recognition in these types of organizations is the responsibility of the local management team. But corporate executives should set aside the time to at least visit each facility or division annually. A facility-wide tour will allow local management to introduce the corporate executives to some of the individuals who participated in making the EDIS a success. A ''nice job'' from a company executive is a simple, but powerful, form of recognition. Word of recognition of this type will spread quickly and will serve as a positive reinforcement to the EDIS.

Management must be careful not to recognize only those ideas that reap large financial savings. Ignoring ideas that don't save a lot of money or that don't end up being implemented will quickly signal organization members that claims that "no idea is a bad idea" just aren't true. Just because an idea or its implementation may not have been successful doesn't mean it's a bad idea. We can still learn from it. We learn ways *not* to do things and paths *not* to take. Unsuccessful ideas help us narrow our improvement focus. Knowing what doesn't work can often lead to ideas that do work. Recognition of ideas, even if they aren't successful, can help motivate people to continue trying.

Celebrating Successes

Recognition comes in many forms, but celebrations are the most visible. While the employees should be the center of attention in celebrations, the full management team should be leading the cheering section. Absence of the top managers at these events weakens their impact. A cameo appearance trivializes the celebration. An active role in the event demonstrates sincere enthusiasm and excitement.

Developing, Administering, and Auditing the Idea System

As Dr. Deming has said, management is responsible for the systems. An EDIS is no different than any other system in the organization. Top management may use an EDIS development team to develop the idea system and a steering committee to administer it, but it is management's role to see that these are done right and done well. This is another area that management simply can't abdicate. As part of developing the system, top management must ensure that the existing processes, such as maintenance, purchasing, accounting, and other support processes, are user friendly. In most organizations, they aren't; instead, they are bureaucratic nightmares that will bog down the entire idea system in red tape. A few encounters with bureaucracy of this kind will put a quick end to an EDIS.

Another role of top management is to define the boundaries of freedom for the idea system. This starts with establishing the boundaries for the EDIS development team and then for the EDIS steering committee. Working with top management, these committees will define the boundaries of freedom for employees participating in the idea system. As mentioned earlier (Chapter 1), it is top management's role to help communicate and clarify these boundaries to the employees. It is the idea system steering committee's role to administer those boundaries of freedom.

Top management should also audit the process from time to time. Using data from the EDIS, plus getting data directly from employees (by talking to them), management can measure the status of the EDIS. The data can show that the idea system is working well throughout the organization; it can also show the idea system may need a shot of adrenaline in some areas to encourage greater participation.

Role of EDIS Steering Committee

In Chapter 5 we talked about the EDIS development team. The development team is the group responsible for the development of the entire system. In some cases, the development team (or some people from it) may become (members of) the EDIS steering committee, steering the system they developed. The EDIS development team is, relatively, a short-term project team. When the EDIS is developed, the team's job is complete and it can disband. For more information on what the development team needs to do, see Chapter 5.

Once the EDIS has been developed and rolled out companywide, the EDIS steering committee assumes the role of providing ongoing guidance. It provides support by:

- assisting the administrator
- visibly promoting the EDIS
- measuring EDIS results
- handling ideas beyond the supervisor's boundaries of freedom

Additional functions of the EDIS steering committee are:

- to help simplify support processes
- provide retraining
- keep the EDIS connected to the TQM Council by providing feedback

Process Simplification

How smooth an EDIS functions normally depends upon the support processes. Among those support functions most critical to the success of EDIS are the maintenance work order process and the purchasing process. Others may include the process to get drawings done by the engineering group, and the capital process. Any process that employees must use to implement their ideas must be reviewed and simplified before an EDIS is kicked off.

The EDIS steering committee may have to work with the functional support groups to simplify the work order and purchasing process. More likely, though, project teams will be assigned to attack these areas. The project teams should report to the EDIS steering committee. The project teams must do three things:

- Simplify
  - Simplify
    - Simplify

If maintenance and purchasing systems are to be simplified, maintenance and purchasing personnel must be on the simplification CI teams. However, they must understand that they have not been cast in the roles of "defenders of the systems." The EDIS steering committee may need to facilitate these projects to ensure that everyone on the simplification teams is working to simplify the processes and are not caught up in a, "Well, that's the way we've always done it," way of thinking.

In a multisite corporation, the one process that might be difficult to simplify prior to implementing an EDIS is the process for getting capital funding. Most large organizations have highly defined capital requisitioning processes. In these cases, simplification may be beyond the reach of the local EDIS steering committee. The steering committee can still work to simplify the local portion of the capital requisitioning process but should not waste effort initially on convincing corporate staffs about the need to simplify this process. The steering committee should focus initially on educating the employees on how the capital process works.

Retraining

Everyone needs to know how an EDIS works, how to participate in it, and how the support-service processes work. All employees need training and refresher training in EDIS basics to contribute. Both supervisors and the top management team will need training in additional areas. Table 6.1 recaps training requirements for a typical organization.

TQM Council Feedback

The EDIS steering committee is a major source of feedback to top management on both the idea system as well as the organization's CI efforts. The EDIS steering committee needs to be open and honest with its feedback. The TQM Council needs to be open to this feedback, and when the feedback requires action, it needs to act.

The EDIS steering committee needs to keep the council abreast of how the idea system is working. This information should be presented to the council on a scheduled basis (e.g., monthly); it should not be subjective in nature. Using visual-data display tools, the results from the EDIS measurement system should be reviewed with the council. A part of this review includes any recommendations that the EDIS steering committee has for the council based on the data collected. This may include recommending that top management encourage more participation from some parts of the organization and that they recognize the areas that are active and effective with the EDIS.

A common area for feedback from the EDIS steering committee to top management is to encourage the top management team to

TABLE 6.1.   EDIS Training Requirements

EVERYONE

- Continuous improvement/problem-solving process
- How to submit an idea
- How to have maintenance done
- How to purchase an item
- Who to go to with a question
- How they'll be recognized
- Boundaries of freedom for ideas

SUPERVISORS

- All of the training for everyone
- How to submit a capital-project request
- How to coach an employee with an idea
- Boundaries of freedom for approving ideas

TOP MANAGEMENT TEAM

- All of the training for everyone
- Summary of training given to supervisors
- Recognition strategies
- Reward methods (e.g., gainsharing)

"walk like they talk"; that is, if they are going to promote EDIS and encourage employees to participate, they themselves must actively participate. It is likely that the EDIS steering committee will hear of problems with the organization's CI Process. Some of these areas may have to be addressed with top management.

The TQM Council also needs feedback on the effectiveness of the recognition and reward strategies. The EDIS steering committee is well positioned to provide feedback on the balance of recognition between individuals and teams and the balance of recognition between departments. (Recognition of teams encourages teamwork; traditionally, we have recognized individuals, not teams.) The steering committee, being "lower to the ground," will likely be the first group to hear about departments, teams, or individuals who feel they have been overlooked by top management while others have gotten all the recognition. Providing this feedback to the TQM Council can help rectify problems before they build.

Supervisor's Role

No role in the EDIS is more pivotal than the supervisor's. With the power to approve most ideas and the responsibility to coach the individuals and teams through the idea-implementation process, the supervisors really determine the success of an EDIS. A supervisor not actively involved in and committed to an EDIS undermines the entire idea system. At a minimum, the undermining exists only in that supervisor's department or group. At worst, it spreads throughout the organization.

Idea Approval

The supervisor approves ideas within boundaries of freedom defined by the EDIS steering committee and the TQM Council. To do this, the supervisor must clearly and completely understand the boundaries. The boundaries define monetary limits, employee time, idea scope (e.g., does the idea cross departments?), and information access. A supervisor unsure of these boundaries must clarify them with the EDIS steering committee.

Two dangerous situations can appear when the supervisor does not know his or her boundaries of freedom. For one, the supervisor can approve an idea and the employee can begin implementation only to have the plug pulled because approval of the idea was beyond the supervisor's authority. This creates instant resentment from the employee, both for the supervisor and the EDIS. Like a consumer who has problems with a purchased item, the employee will "save" coworkers from EDIS by broadcasting how poorly the idea system works.

In the second case, a supervisor who pictures the boundaries of freedom too narrowly will be a burden to an EDIS. This supervisor kicks up too many ideas to the steering committee, bogging down the entire process, discouraging employees from participating in the EDIS, and slowing the system down to a crawl. The end result is frustrated employees.

The Supervisor as an Idea Coach

Coaching an individual or team through the EDIS process may involve:

- clarifying boundaries of freedom
- assisting in developing and refining ideas
- directing employees to needed resources
- facilitating removal of roadblocks
- encouraging teamwork

Not all ideas are applicable for implementation. Every idea submitted to the supervisor is an important one to the person submitting it. As an idea coach, the supervisor must work with the idea maker(s) to develop an idea, to bring out the best in it.

Another coaching role is to direct employees to the resources they need to develop and implement their ideas. In order to do this, the supervisor must know the organization and know the processes critical to an EDIS (e.g., purchasing and maintenance systems). In a large organization, getting all of the supervisors to the point of knowing where to direct an idea maker for assistance on his or her idea can be difficult. (One method to minimize this is to develop a decision-making flowchart that details where in the organization to go for specific support services. This should be available to everyone, not just the supervisors.)

Roadblocks often crop up that make it difficult or impossible for an idea maker to develop and implement an idea. These roadblocks may include:

- problems getting support services or in getting realistic commitment dates from them
- an idea that creates conflicts between shifts or between employees
- "Turf-dom," where a group or department drags its feet because they believe an idea infringes on its area of responsibility
- lack of a timely response from the EDIS steering committee and/or top management on ideas requiring their approval
- procrastination on the part of the idea maker

Many other potential roadblocks can and will arise. The supervisors must have the persistence to help the idea maker overcome these roadblocks and successfully implement the idea.

American culture is one of rugged individualism. Teamwork does not come naturally to many people. Yet teamwork is becoming more and more essential for organizations wanting to remain competitive. It is absolutely critical to the success of an EDIS. The supervisor in the EDIS must instill a team environment in the department or group and work to maintain teamwork among departments. When an employee or team creates an improvement idea, the supervisor must encourage teamwork and, in some cases, *insist* on teamwork. We can't have people working on improvement ideas in a vacuum; the end result may be good only for the individual and not for the team.

Role of the Union

Unions were formed early in the twentieth century to protect workers from unfair management practices. Management expected workers to show up, do the job whatever the conditions, and not ask any questions or register any complaints. Workers organized mainly to obtain fair wages and safer working conditions. Today, with federal wage and safety regulations, the need for unions has declined. However, many organizations remain unionized, and in these organizations the union has an important role to play in any EDIS. The union role includes:

- Participating on the EDIS steering committee
- Helping supervisors redefine their role as idea coach
- Encouraging employees to take an active role in their jobs
- Encouraging teamwork
- Helping save jobs

Union Participation on the EDIS Development Team and Steering Committee

The role of the EDIS development team is to create an effective idea system. The role of the EDIS steering committee is to administer the idea system and to encourage participation from throughout the organization. To accomplish these objectives, the development team and the steering committee both need their membership to reflect the breadth and depth of the organization. Regardless of the organization, unionized or nonunionized, the EDIS development team and steering committee need representation from the top of the organization down to the worker level. They need the viewpoint of the workers. This viewpoint will make the entire EDIS process run more smoothly and garner greater participation.

Union representatives do not have to be members of the union committee or a shop steward. In fact, in most organizations, they are not the best participants by far. The ideal participants from a union are the same as the ideal participants from the worker level in any organization—the informal leaders in the facility. These are the people who are regarded in a positive light by their peers, whom others turn to with questions and earn their respect when they speak. Employees with negative attitudes are not wanted on the EDIS steering committee; this is not a place to try to turn around someone with a negative attitude.

Union members of the EDIS steering committee are not there to play the role of the police. They are on the steering committee to help develop and administer the idea system. They are not there to renegotiate contractual items by reviewing an idea against the bargaining agreement. Contractual issues must be left to the union committee-management team for resolution.

Helping Supervisors Redefine Roles

For many supervisors, changing roles will be difficult. Habits of many years will not change overnight. However, people will expect that they will. As an organization implements EDIS, there will be complaints about some of the supervisors. It's inevitable. When this occurs, the union should not jump on the bandwagon. Instead, the union should work with the EDIS steering committee to help the supervisors redefine their roles. Part of this involves the union providing positive feedback and recognition to supervisors for even the small things that they are doing right to help employees implement their improvement ideas.

Encourage Employees to Take an Active Role

An EDIS gives everyone in an organization the opportunity to improve the quality of its products and processes, and the quality of their work life. Some employees will be reluctant at first to participate in the EDIS. Some will continue to register complaints with the union committee to secure action. For organizations in an EDIS environment, the union committee can get out of the middle of noncontract items. Often, if someone has a complaint, they also have an idea to correct the situation. By having the person redirect his or her complaint/improvement idea into the idea system, the union committee will be an "enabler" in a positive sense; they will enable that person to take an active role in his or her job and the quality of their work life.

Encourage Teamwork

In manufacturing organizations, maintenance workers are often viewed as prima donnas by the production workers. Each shift views themselves as better than the others. In service organizations, similar factors exist. A union can play a major role in minimizing or eliminating friction between departments, groups, and individuals. If people are going to continue to have the opportunity to improve the quality of their work and their working environment, then the union must encourage teamwork among its membership and among everyone in the organization. EDIS depends on this teamwork. It will not survive in any organization where factions constantly fight and bicker.

Save Jobs

This sounds simplistic; it sounds idealistic. But if a union and its members participate on the EDIS steering committee, help supervisors to change their roles, encourage employees to take an active role in their jobs, and encourage teamwork, then the net result will be a more efficient, more competitive organization. This can save jobs from being lost to domestic or overseas competitors; saving jobs is one of the founding principles of unions. A more efficient, more competitive organization may also grow, creating the need for new jobs and, in a union environment, more union members.

Everyone's Role

With an EDIS in place, everyone in the organization should be:

- coming up with improvement ideas;
- implementing their ideas using teamwork within departments, between departments, and between shifts.

The key here is *everyone*. EDIS is not just for first-line workers. It is for *all* workers, from the first line right up to the CEO. It's everyone's responsibility to say to themselves, *"It's never good enough!"* and then to constantly find ways of improving their jobs and organizations by implementing their improvement ideas.

Chapter 7

Using Continuous Improvement Tools to Generate Ideas

An effective Employee-Driven Idea System (EDIS) revolves around the concept of Employee Empowerment. As outlined in Chapter 1, empowerment stems from employees working in the right environment and having the tools of continuous improvement (CI). Without the right environment or without the proper tools, employees cannot take the initiative to make improvements in their processes. An EDIS cannot survive if either situation is present.

We've spent a great deal of this book discussing creating the environment for establishing an EDIS. We haven't really discussed CI tools as they relate to an idea system. Yet many of the same CI tools that we use on project teams and in other total quality (TQ) activities have important roles in an EDIS. We can use CI tools to:

1. Identify areas needing improvement ideas
2. Generate ideas both as individuals and groups
3. Select ideas to work on

4. Help refine ideas
5. Present ideas for approval
6. Implement ideas

Table 7.1 summarizes some of the CI tools that can be used in these areas. The remainder of this chapter will focus on describing these tools and some of their applications in an EDIS.

TABLE 7.1.   Summary of CI Tools for EDIS

1. Tools to Identify Areas Needing Improvement Ideas

• Pareto Diagrams	• Data-Presentation Techniques
• Flowcharts	• Two-Dimensional Surveys
• Workflow Diagrams	• Benchmarking
• Histograms	• FMEA
• Control Charts	• Fault-Tree Analysis
• Concentration Diagrams	

2. Tools for Generating Ideas

For use with individuals or groups:

• Five Whys	• Brown-Paper Flowcharts
• Internal-Customer Surveys	• Flowcharts
• Workflow Diagrams	• Benchmarking

For use with groups:
• Brainstorming
• CEDAC

3. Tools for Selecting Ideas to Work On

• Pareto Diagrams	• Voting and Ranking
• Cause-and-Effect Diagrams	• Affinity Diagrams

(continued)

TABLE 7.1. Continued

4. Tools for Refining Ideas

- Internal-Customer Surveys
- Cause-and-Effect Diagrams
- Affinity Diagrams

5. Tools for Presenting Ideas for Approval

Data-Presentation Techniques

- Histograms
- Bar Graphs
- Pie Charts
- Line Graphs
- Concentration Diagrams
- Scatter Diagrams
- Tally Sheets
- Trend Charts

Showing the Process Flow

- Flowcharts
- Workflow Diagrams
- Brown-paper Flowcharts

6. Tools for Implementing Ideas

- Checklists
- PERT Charts
- Activity Plans

Tools to Identify Areas Needing Improvement Ideas

Employees will easily come up with improvement ideas when the EDIS first kicks off. Later, ideas may not come as easily to them. Just like it's easier to pick the low-hanging fruit in an orchard, employee's ideas will initially be the easy, obvious ideas they probably have been thinking about for years. But eventually all the low-hanging fruit will be picked, and it's tougher to get to the fruit higher in the trees. It's the same with ideas; employees will have to stretch to find more opportunities for improvement. Some CI tools readily lend themselves to this job:

- Pareto Diagrams
- Flowcharts
- Workflow Diagrams
- Histograms
- Control Charts
- Concentration Diagrams
- Simple Data-Presentation Techniques
- Two-Dimensional Surveys
- Benchmarking
- Failure Mode and Effect Analysis
- Fault-Tree Analysis

Employees who have been trained in the CI tools will find them helpful in identifying improvement areas. The EDIS steering committee can also use the tools to focus employees on a theme of the month tied to a specific process, product, or area of the organization.

The Pareto Diagram

A Pareto diagram helps us to focus on the vital few problems or areas for improvement rather than the trivial many. The Pareto diagram (Figure 7.1) is a combination bar graph/line chart that presents data in descending order of importance. This allows us to focus our efforts on the few items that contribute to the bulk of the problem. In Figure 7.1, the first three items account for 69 percent of the total expenses for the month. We would want to look for savings in these three areas rather than the others. Savings in these three areas will have the greatest impact on our overall expense reduction program.

To help employees focus, a few of the areas Pareto diagrams could be constructed for are:

- Department safety performance
- Cost of quality by product
- Equipment downtime
- Product problems
- Errors on forms
- Costs for supplies
- Department costs

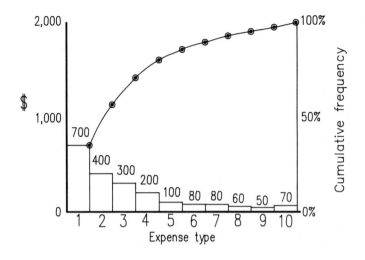

Expense type   1 Rent   6 Clothes
                           2 Food   7 Entertainment
                           3 Car payment   8 Gas
                           4 Taxes   9 Savings
                           5 Electricity/heat   10 All other

FIGURE 7.1. Pareto Diagram

Flowcharts

Flowcharts visually present the activity and decision steps needed to complete a process. A flowchart (Figure 7.2) of the overall process for delivering a product or service may point to areas in the process or to departments that need to be improved. The EDIS steering committee can use this information to ask employees to focus on improvement ideas in those areas.

Workflow Diagrams

Workflow diagrams show the physical path that a product, service, and even paperwork takes as it is completed. In Figure 7.3, we can see that the data-processing department is the area to focus our im-

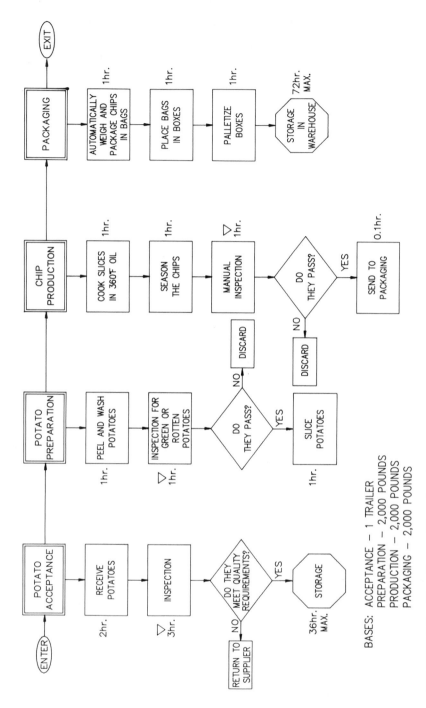

FIGURE 7.2. Top Down Flowchart

142

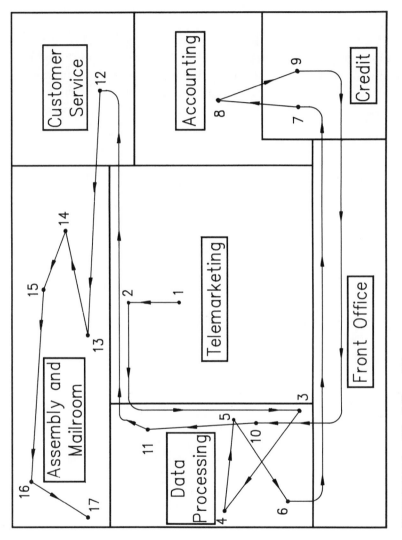

FIGURE 7.3. Workflow Diagram

provement efforts because of the criss-crossing of the paperwork flow paths.

Histograms

We often get reams of data in tables or in computer printouts. It is hard to do anything with this data. We have to search through it for the highest values, the lowest values, and the most typical values. This search is usually very time consuming and frequently inaccurate.

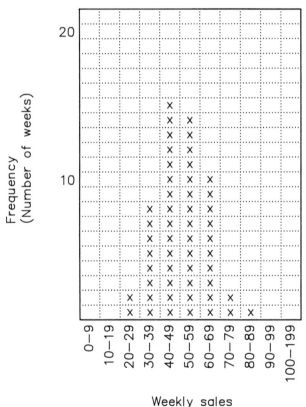

Weekly sales
(Hundreds of gallons of gasoline)

FIGURE 7.4.   Histogram

Data analysis would be much easier if we could see the variation in the process. A histogram (Figure 7.4), also known as a frequency distribution, puts data into the form of a picture. It shows us the pattern of variation in a process. This tool can be used to identify processes that produce "outliers" (outcomes that are very different from the rest). The EDIS steering committee can ask employees to specifically look for ideas from these processes.

A histogram is used with characteristics that can be measured on a variable scale. The X axis represents the value of the characteristic and the Y axis the frequency (number of times a measurement has occurred). An X is placed in the appropriate column each time a value occurs. In Figure 7.4, 4000 to 4999 gallons were sold 15 times. On only one occasion were 8000 to 8999 gallons sold.

Control Charts

When organizations want to monitor and statistically control their processes, they use control charts. Control charts (Figure 7.5) are used to monitor the process and identity when the process has gone out of control so that action can be taken to eliminate the special cause of variation. Taking action is important. Sometimes, the action fixes the problem temporarily and doesn't get to the root cause. In these cases, a team may be assigned to investigate the problem. If the team is unsuccessful in finding the root cause, then the EDIS steering committee may post copies of the control chart and request improvement ideas from the employees working in the area.

Concentration Diagrams

Concentration diagrams literally make a picture out of our problems. They show us where problems are concentrated. Figure 7.6 shows a concentration diagram in a hotel. An X shows the location of every customer complaint about (lack of) cleanliness. For the hotel, this diagram can be used to get employees to think of ideas for improving methods for cleaning the tub area because that's where the complaints are concentrated. A concentration diagram for yield losses or

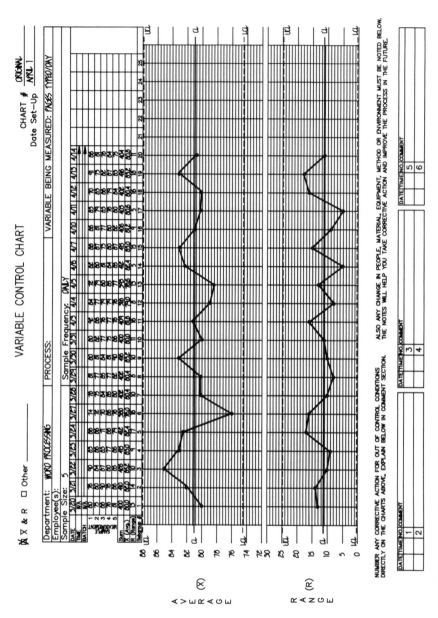

FIGURE 7.5. Control Chart

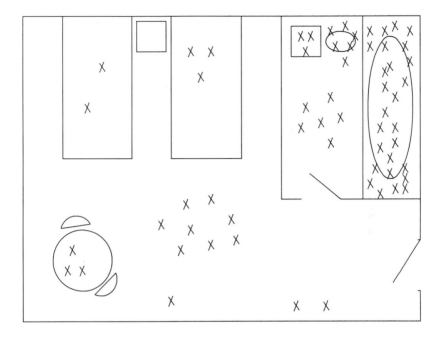

FIGURE 7.6. Concentration Diagram

accidents or other problems may help focus employees' improvement ideas on the key problem areas.

Simple Data-Presentation Techniques

Simple data-presentation techniques such as line graphs (Figure 7.7), bar charts (Figure 7.8), pie charts (Figure 7.9), scatter diagrams (Figure 7.10), and trend charts (Figure 7.11) can help identify improvement opportunities. We use line graphs and bar graphs to view similar features of different items or processes. Pie charts show what percentage of the whole each item makes up. Scatter diagrams show if there is any relationship between two variables or two characteristics in our process. We can see how a characteristic changes over time with a trend chart. All of these data-presentation techniques can help give us clues on where to focus our improvement efforts so that the

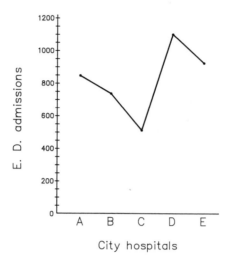

FIGURE 7.7.   Line Graph

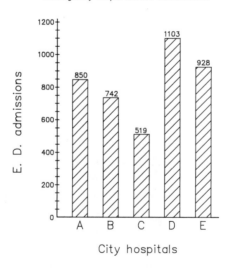

FIGURE 7.8.   Bar Chart

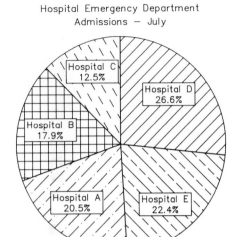

FIGURE 7.9.   Pie Chart

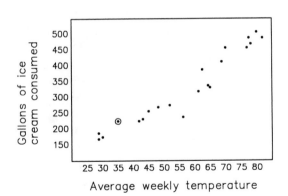

FIGURE 7.10.   Scatter Diagram

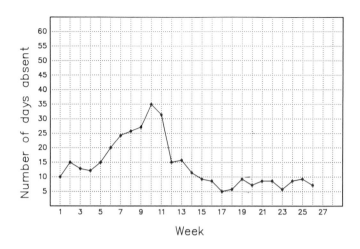

FIGURE 7.11.   Trend Chart

EDIS steering committee can ask employees to look for improvement ideas in the areas needing them.

Two-Dimensional Surveys

Most surveys only ask our customers or our employees about how we perform in certain areas. They only survey one dimension; they don't ask about the importance of each area. A two-dimensional survey asks about both performance and importance. If we rate both the performance and importance on scales of 1 to 4 (with ''4'' being best performance and essential), we can graphically display the results for each survey question on a two-dimensional scatter diagram (Figure 7.12). A two-dimensional scatter diagram can show us where we have poor performance on items essential to the customer or our employees (majority of points in quadrant 4, Q4), areas where we have good performance in essential items (Q1), poor performance in unimportant areas (Q3), and good performance in unimportant areas (Q2). We can take the average results from all questions and plot them by question number on a summary sheet (Figure 7.13). Using this summary sheet, we can set priorities (Q4, Q1, Q2, Q3) and focus employees to come up with ideas for the areas needing them most.

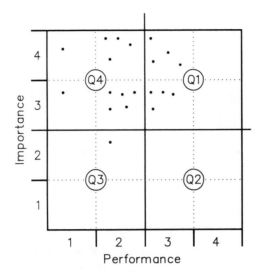

FIGURE 7.12. Two-Dimensional Survey Scatter Diagram

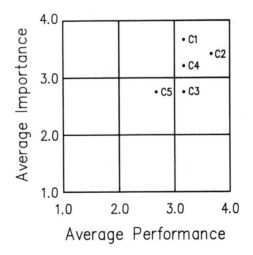

Note:
C1=Category 1, C2=Category 2, ...

FIGURE 7.13. Two-Dimensional Survey Summary Data Sheet

Two-dimensional surveys can be used with external customers on:

- Product performance
- Cost of ownership
- Product features
- On-time delivery
- Ease in dealing with us

Customers' feedback can point employees to specific areas in need of improvements.

Benchmarking

Benchmarking is the process of determining industry or "world" best practices and then studying them to identify areas for improvement within our organization. For example, Xerox Corporation benchmarked the warehousing operations of L.L. Bean as part of the effort to improve their distribution of Xerox products. Benchmarking can help identify specific practices that need improvement. After identifying these practices, an organization can provide this information to employees to solicit specific ideas for improvements via the EDIS. Benchmarking is a six-step process involving the following.

1. Set Up the Team

A benchmarking team should have two to four members. The team members may be from the same department but it would be better if they were not. Having members from different departments and even different levels in the organization, will bring a different perspective to the team and may enable the team to do a better job benchmarking.

Once the team has been selected, the roles of the individuals must be defined. A team leader should be chosen if one was not selected by the EDIS steering committee or top management. Other roles such as scribe should also be defined by the team.

Team ground rules should be defined in the first team meeting.

These ground rules should cover how often the team will meet and for how long, how disagreements will be handled, and what the team's boundaries of freedom are, among other topics.

2. Clarify the (Benchmarking) Objective

This involves identifying the practice or process for benchmarking. These may include relations with suppliers, customer-service activities, telemarketing, warehousing, waste disposal, and many others. Once this is identified, the team should then construct a flowchart of their existing process and walk through it to ensure all team members understand it the same way. This is a valuable reference point for the team later when actually benchmarking.

3. Find the Targets to Benchmark

The best target for benchmarking information on a specific practice is an organization renowned in the industry or as a "world best" in that practice. Trade publications and professional societies can help identify these organizations. These sources may also be the only way to acquire competitive benchmarking data.

4. Identify the Performance Gaps

Contact the target benchmark organization and determine if they truly are a benchmark. If they are, arrange to visit them to study the practice of interest. One method of getting acceptance for a benchmarking visit is to offer a "trade." Choose something that your organization does well and share information on it. Benchmarking works best when it's a two-way street. The entire benchmarking team should go on the visit, if possible. A single person should never go on a benchmarking visit. A benchmarking team is more likely not to miss importance information.

During the visit, the team should look for gaps between their performance and the benchmark's. They should also be looking for reasons for these gaps. The reasons may give the team ideas for improving their practices or processes.

5. Develop and Implement the Action (Improvement) Plan

Careful planning needs to take place once the benchmarking team returns. One result of benchmarking is specific improvement ideas. The benchmarking team can work with the EDIS steering committee to decide which ideas the team will work on and which will be assigned to other teams or individuals for action. Care must be taken so that *who* will do *what* by *when* is clear for each idea to be worked on.

The benchmarking team's visit may not result in specific improvement ideas. It may only be able to identify areas that need improvement. These areas can be turned over to the EDIS steering committee to roll out to the employees to help focus their ideas.

6. Evaluate and Adjust

With the completion of all of the ideas, the benchmarking team should get back together and compare the results obtained with what they saw at the benchmark. They should make recommendations for any adjustments that need to be made to further improve the practice or process.

FMEA—Failure Mode and Effects Analysis

FMEA got its start as a tool to improve safety. It has evolved into a tool to improve almost any area of a business by determining how a process might fail. The failure modes are prioritized based on the effects those failures will have. The EDIS steering committee can then focus employees on those areas needing improvement.

FMEA involves a team of employees brainstorming for the failure modes that could possibly occur in the process.

The team then analyzes these failure modes. These failure modes are prioritized by calculating a relative-risk value that is based on the team's ratings of the frequency of the failure mode, the severity of the effect should the failure mode occur, and the likelihood of detecting the failure mode. The ratings for frequency, severity, and detection are agreed to by the team on a 1–10 scale. The relative risk is calculated by multiplying these three ratings (for a maximum relative risk of 1,000).

Once the relative risks for each of the failure modes are calculated, the EDIS steering committee can post the vital few (those with the highest risk), and request ideas on how to reduce the relative risk. Risk reduction can be accomplished by reducing the frequency of occurrence, reducing the severity of the effect should the failure mode occur, or increasing the likelihood of detection. Mistake-proofing is the best tool for reducing the relative risk. Figure 7.14 shows a page from a completed FMEA.

Fault-Tree Analysis

Like FMEA, fault-tree analysis has historically been a safety-improvement tool. And like FMEA, it can be used in CI efforts. Fault-tree analysis starts with a team identifying safety and quality faults (failures) that could occur in the process. Then, the team branches its way inside the process to identify potential root causes of these faults (Figure 7.15). Preventive measures should be put in place to ensure these root causes cannot recur. This might require a collective focus on the root cause and the EDIS steering committee can point employees in the direction where their ideas are needed.

Tools for Generating Ideas

Although employees will typically come up with ideas on their own, there are CI tools that can help them generate more and better ideas. Some of these tools are the same ones mentioned before as tools for identifying areas needing improvement ideas such as surveys, workflow diagrams, flowcharts, and benchmarking. There are others that can be used by individual or groups to generate improvement ideas.

Five Whys

This is a technique for getting to the root cause of a problem. It is useful for individuals or teams to help them work through a problem to generate an improvement idea aimed at eliminating the root cause. As Figure 7.16 shows, the five whys act like a microscope focusing in closer and closer to the root cause. We ask "why" until we zero in.

Process: Riding Mower Assembly Line
Team Name: Nuts 'n bolts
Team Leader: Kevin B.

Date Initiated: 15 Dec
Date Completed: 6 Mar

FAILURE MODE	EFFECTS OF FAILURE	F	S	D	RISK	ACTION REQUIRED	DONE	REVISED RATINGS				FURTHER ACTION NEEDED
								F	S	D	RISK	
• Rear wiring harness gets pinched in muffler assembly	• Wires may get cut during use: —electrical system shorts —rear lights won't work —turn signals won't work —brake lights won't work	8	6	10	480	• Change design of wire path to inside of the seat well	✓	—	—	—	—	• No
• Safety switch under seat wired backwards	• Mower will not start when someone is seated; will start without anyone on the seat	4	8	7	224	• Change connector design to only fit one way • No	✓	—	—	—	—	• No
• Tires misaligned in rear	• Excessive tire wear • Reduced gas mileage	7	4	1	28							
• Loose ignition switch	• Difficulty in starting the mower	10	7	7	490	• Worked with supplier to lengthen thread	✓	2	7	7	98	• No

FIGURE 7.14. A Page From a Completed FMEA

Fault Tree Analysis – Cold Mill Area

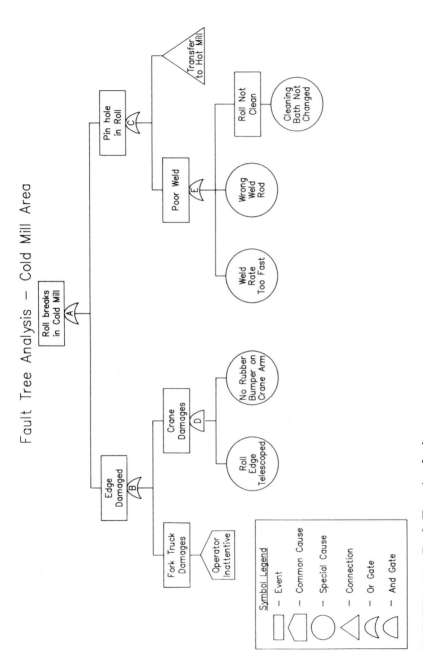

FIGURE 7.15. Fault-Tree Analysis

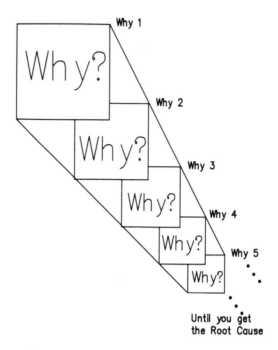

Why 1

Why 2

Why 3

Why 4

Why 5

Until you get
the Root Cause

FIGURE 7.16. Visualizing the Five Whys

Let's look at an example to show this technique. The example involves a problem in making potato chips; the saltiness of the chips varied too much from one chip to another in a manufacturer's new process.

1. Why does the saltiness vary so much from one chip to another? *Because the salt applicator doesn't feed consistently.*
2. Why doesn't the salt applicator feed consistently? *Because the feed screw doesn't give a steady stream of salt to the applicator.*
3. Why doesn't the feed screw give a steady stream of salt? *Because the salt bridges in its storage hopper.*
4. Why does the salt bridge in the storage hopper? *Because the hopper walls are not steep enough.*
5. Why aren't the hopper walls steep enough? *Because of the properties of the salt itself.*

Actually, after our fourth why, we should have been able to come up with ideas to solve the root cause of the problem. Our idea could be installing a bridge-breaker in the hopper or even redesigning the hopper. (It's unlikely that we can change the properties of the salt itself.) The term five whys is just a term; sometimes we'll need to ask why more than five times to get to the root cause, sometimes less. The key thing is not to stop until we've gotten to the root cause. Once the root cause is determined, it is usually easy to come up with an idea for eliminating the root cause. The individual or group can put the idea into EDIS and take action on it within their boundaries of freedom.

Internal Customer Surveys

Customer surveys are described in the previous section. In order to generate improvement ideas when conducting an internal customer survey, we have to ask not only about our performance and its importance, but must also ask open-ended questions on how we can improve our products and services. From the responses we can often come up with improvement ideas that can be monitored and implemented through EDIS.

Workflow Diagram

A workflow diagram (Figure 7.17) shows the actual paths taken by paperwork and individuals performing services. Constructing a workflow diagram involves taking a floor plan or a sketch (to scale) of the building and equipment layout and drawing in the paths. The amount of time taken by each path can also be drawn in. This view of a process can lead to many view ideas on improving equipment layout (both manufacturing and office equipment), on bringing needed tools (even tools such as files) to where needed, and on eliminating duplication efforts. Figure 7.18 shows how the flow for making pizzas in a restaurant was improved with just ideas from a workflow diagram. Employees or groups can put their ideas for improving the flow of work in their processes into EDIS for implementation.

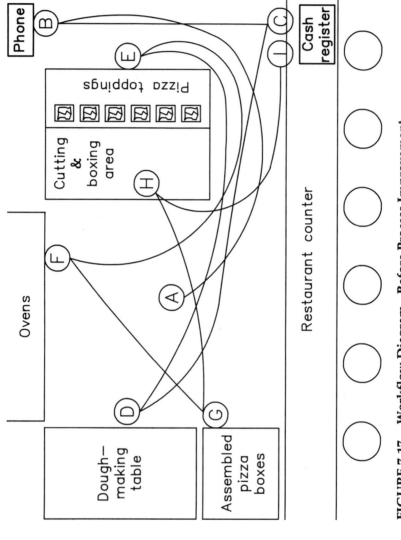

FIGURE 7.17. Workflow Diagram—Before Process Improvement

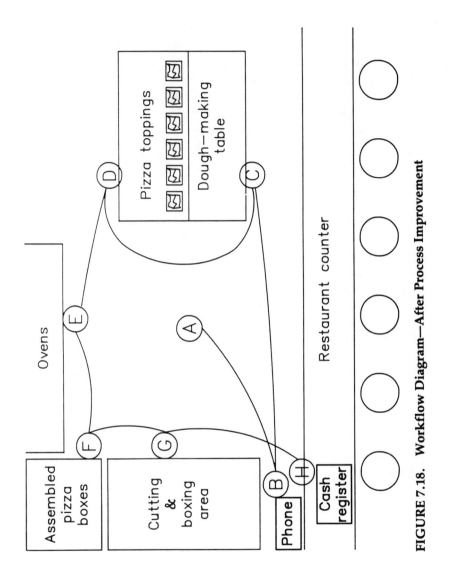

FIGURE 7.18. Workflow Diagram—After Process Improvement

Flowcharts

Flowcharts are described in a previous section. We can use flowcharts to come up with immediate improvement ideas by looking for ways to combine or eliminate activity steps, eliminate decision points, and turn decision points into activities.

A brown-paper flowchart is a special form of a flowchart. It is created by taking all of the paperwork from a process and laying it out on brown kraft paper. This helps generate ideas on where paperwork and data collection duplication exists so as to eliminate it. It may also give an idea on where important information from the process is missing.

Benchmarking

Benchmarking was described in the previous section. We can generate many improvement ideas just as a result of comparing our processes with the benchmark's processes and their practices.

Brainstorming

This is a group technique for generating a large number of ideas. A brainstorming session can quickly yield 40 or more improvement ideas in an organized fashion that allows everyone in the group to participate. The goal of brainstorming is to identify more and better ideas by using many heads rather than one; often, one person's idea will trigger another person to improve upon the original idea or to come up with a radically new idea to solve the root cause of the problem.

We recommend round-robin brainstorming where everyone gets a turn over free-wheeling brainstorming where people just throw out ideas at will. Free-wheeling brainstorming is often dominated by a few individuals, and can easily be taken off course from the brainstorming objective set by the group or by the EDIS steering committee.

The rules for round-robin brainstorming are straightforward:

1. Have one person lead the session and write down the ideas on a flipchart.
2. Write the objective of the brainstorming session on the flipchart or in a visible location.
3. Go around the room giving each person a chance to contribute an idea.
4. A person may only give one idea per turn.
5. If a person does not have an idea, he or she may pass for this round. They are still participants, however, and may have ideas later as the brainstorming continues.
6. No one may comment on, praise, or criticize any idea. Questions to clarify an idea are allowed. Sarcastic questions *are not* welcome.
7. As the session leader fills up flipchart pages, they should be posted so that everyone can see all the ideas.
8. When everyone passes, the brainstorming session is over.

Not all of the ideas from the brainstorming will be practical (useful), feasible (able to be done), and cost-effective. The group should sort their ideas into 3 classes:

Class 1: Ideas that are practical, feasible, cost-effective, and can be done by the group (within the EDIS boundaries of freedom).

Class 2: Ideas that are practical, feasible, and cost-effective but are outside the group's boundaries of freedom; these ideas are for the EDIS steering committee or the TQM Council to consider.

Class 3: Ideas that are not practical, feasible, or cost-effective at this time. These ideas should be recorded on paper, but nothing should be done with them for the time being.

Once the ideas are sorted, the group can divide up the class 1 ideas and do them under EDIS. Class 2 ideas should be forwarded to the EDIS steering committee for its consideration. Some of these may be returned for someone in the group to implement. Others may be forwarded to top management for approval.

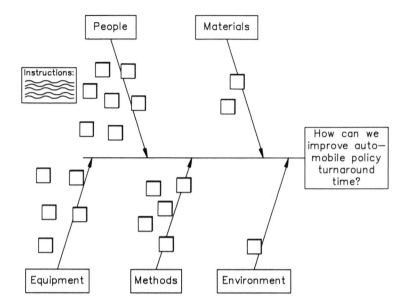

**FIGURE 7.19.   CEDAC Cards Added to the Cause
and Effect Diagram**

CEDAC[1]

CEDAC (Figure 7.19) stands for cause and effect diagram with the addition of cards. It is a visual technique to capture ideas to solve a specific problem or improve any situation. In many ways, CEDAC is a slow brainstorming process. Employees are encouraged to add cards with their ideas onto a large cause and effect (CE diagram) that has been posted in a conspicuous place in the area that improvement ideas are needed.

The EDIS steering committee may select area/improvement targets where CEDAC may be useful. The steering committee should not, however, be the CEDAC champion. CEDAC can generate a large number of improvement ideas. As these ideas are anonymous, the steering committee will bog itself down if it becomes the "owner" of

---

[1]CEDAC is a trademark held by Productivity Press, Inc.

the CEDAC and the ideas it generates. To avoid this problem, once the EDIS steering committee has targeted an area for CEDAC, they should have a team to champion it. The team can put up the CEDAC chart, publicize it, sort through the ideas generated, and champion the best of the ideas themselves.

To use CEDAC to generate ideas, the CEDAC team should post a large CE diagram (Figure 7.20) in a conspicuous location. Based on discussion with the EDIS steering committee, the desired improvement should be written into the effect box on the CE diagram. Alongside the CEDAC, the team should post a pad of self-stick notes, a pencil, and instructions on how to participate in the CEDAC. The CEDAC should be publicized and left up for at least a week (but not more than two to three weeks). At that point the team should sort out ideas that are not practical, feasible, or cost-effective. The remaining ideas should be prioritized with a technique such as voting or ranking and then entered into the EDIS with a team member (or the idea generator, if known) listed as champion.

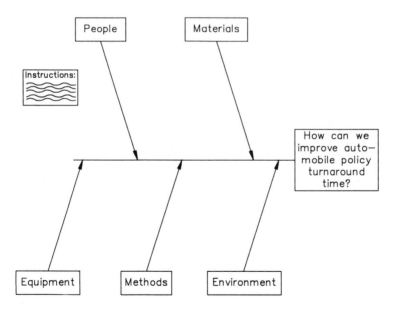

FIGURE 7.20. Cause and Effect Diagram as Basis for CEDAC Chart

Tools for Selecting Ideas to Work On

The EDIS should result in many ideas being generated and implemented by employees. Some of these ideas will be beyond the boundaries of freedom established for the employees. These ideas will be referred to the EDIS steering committee or up to top management for approval. If there are many ideas in this category, then the steering committee (or top management) will need to use some of the tools of continuous improvement to select which ideas to work on and which idea to work on first.

One of the key tools to use is the Pareto diagram, which was described earlier. This shows the vital few areas where ideas are needed so that an idea for one of these areas can be given a higher priority based on its financial impact. Payback and return on investment (ROI) are two common financial calculations.

Other CI tools for selecting ideas to work on are voting and ranking, cause-and-effect diagrams, and affinity diagrams.

Voting and Ranking

Hard data may not always be available to help the EDIS steering committee select ideas from the pool of ideas kicked up to them. When this occurs, the steering committee must use its collective knowledge to subjectively select the ideas to work on. Voting and ranking is a tool to select ideas by giving participants points to assign to the ideas they think are best. This technique doesn't create hard facts but it does generate a group consensus on which ideas to work on first.

To vote and rank, each participant must give a certain number of points to the ideas he or she thinks are the best. The number of points each person can assign to their favorite ideas depends on the number of ideas there are to vote on. Table 7.2 shows how points should be assigned. For example, if there are five ideas to choose from, each person will give three points to the idea they feel is the best and one point to the second-best idea. They will give nothing to the other ideas. This doesn't mean these other ideas are bad, only that they're not the best.

If there are more than 15 ideas being voted on, then the EDIS

TABLE 7.2. Voting and Ranking Points

Total number of ideas:	4 to 6	7 to 10	11 to 15
Each person picks:	**2 ideas**	**3 ideas**	**4 ideas**
First choice	3 points	5 points	7 points
Second choice	1 point	3 points	5 points
Third choice	N/A	1 point	3 points
Fourth choice	N/A	N/A	1 point

steering committee should stop for a moment to reflect on a couple of questions:

- Are the boundaries of freedom established too tight for the organization? If the EDIS steering committee is getting a high proportion of the ideas kicked up to it, then maybe the boundaries are too restrictive.
- Are we being too lazy to collect data? Voting and ranking is a tool to be used only when no data is available. It's unlikely that there will be more than a handful of ideas where we can't get some data to help make the decision.

Once everyone votes for the ideas they think are best, the points are totaled for each idea. An example is shown in Table 7.3.

TABLE 7.3. Voting and Ranking Example

IDEA	Kevin	Tyler	Shane	K.C.	Sum of All Points	% of Total Points
Staggered lunches	0	3	1	1	5	31.3
Single line	3	0	3	3	9	56.3
Separate business line	1	0	0	0	1	6.3
Express lane	0	1	0	0	1	6.3
Take a number	0	0	0	0	0	0
Total	4	4	4	4	16	100.2*

*Note that the total is 100.2 percent. Of course, we only have 100 percent. The 0.2 percent is due to errors introduced by rounding.

Cause-and-Effect Diagram (CE Diagram)

As mentioned earlier under our description of CEDAC, the CE diagram (Figure 7.21) is a visual technique that shows how causes (the idea) relate to the effect (in this case an improvement). The CE diagram typically organizes ideas into five categories:

1. People
2. Methods
3. Equipment
4. Materials
5. Environment

These categories can be referred to as PMEME[2] (p-me-me). A CE diagram is meant to organize many ideas such as might come from a brainstorming session. Unless the EDIS steering committee has more than 15 ideas, there is little need for a CE diagram.

By breaking down a group of ideas into these categories (or others if they are more appropriate) and then putting the ideas into the form of a picture, the EDIS steering committee may be able to see relationships between ideas. Seeing these relationships will help the steering committee either select areas or ideas to have worked on or to identify where more data is needed from the processes. The latter will, in turn, help the steering committee select ideas to act on.

The first step to creating a CE diagram is to sort the idea into the PMEME categories. One approach to this is to write all the ideas on self-stick notes and post five flipchart sheets on the wall with the PMEME categories written on each. The participants can take each idea and decide which category it should be in.

Once each of the ideas is placed in a category, then the group should look at the sheets one at a time to group similar ideas within the category. With this done, the construction of the CE diagram can begin.

---

[2]The term PMEME was coined by the CI training team at Bettmann Photo Archives, New York, NY.

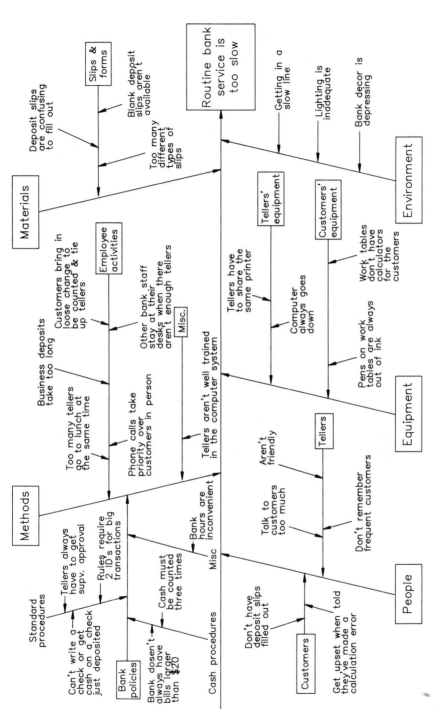

FIGURE 7.21. Conventional Cause and Effect Diagram

169

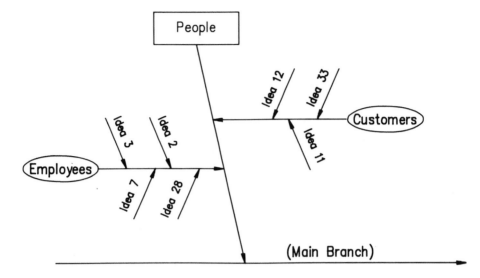

FIGURE 7.22.   Secondary Branches from a Cause and Effect Diagram

1. Draw the trunk of the diagram with the improvement objective (the effect) written in a box on the right side.
2. Draw five main branches representing the PMEME categories.
3. Take the five flipchart pages one at a time and draw in secondary branches for each of the groups of ideas or for any individual ideas. Label the group secondary branches with a group description and then write the ideas in the group as sub-branches off of the secondary branches as show in Figure 7.22.
4. Finally, write in a brief description of all of the individual ideas on their secondary branches.

Affinity Diagram

Like the CE diagram, an affinity diagram is simply a tool to organize a large number of ideas into groups. Once the ideas are organized into the groups, relationships among ideas may be seen so that the EDIS steering committee can select appropriate ideas or groups of ideas to work on. An affinity diagram is shown in Figure 7.23.

The construction of an affinity diagram starts the same way as a

CE diagram, all of the ideas are written down on self-stick notes. The ideas are then stuck randomly on a wall or a table. As a team, the EDIS steering committee should silently look for ideas that they think are related to one another. They should move related ideas together until they have put all of the ideas in four to eight groups.

One of the goals of an affinity diagram is to complete the sorting process quickly. This forces participants to become creative because they must go with their instincts to come up with the related groups of ideas. The silence keeps this process on track by eliminating verbal discussions, persuasions, and disagreements. If someone disagrees with the grouping of one idea with others, they simply move it.

Not all ideas will be grouped with others. These lone ideas are left alone. Once the steering committee has settled on the groups, they should look for one idea from the group that best describes the group. This idea would become the group heading. If no idea is appropriate for the group heading, then the team should come up with a short description of the group to serve as a heading. After headings have been selected for all of the groups, the ideas can be transferred onto the final affinity diagram. Similar groups should be placed together. With the final affinity diagram, the EDIS steering committee has another tool to help them select ideas to work on.

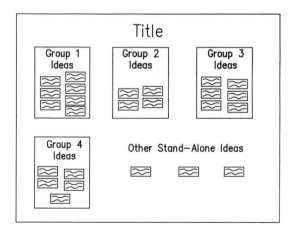

FIGURE 7.23. Affinity Diagram

Tools for Refining Ideas

Many individuals shrink from putting ideas forward because they feel their ideas are still rough and unpolished. They want to wait until they've "thought it through" and refined the idea. Often, the idea never gets acted on further by the individual. An idea that may have been important with just a little modification quickly becomes a lost idea.

There are several tools available to help individuals refine their ideas before they're lost. Three were mentioned in the previous sections: CEDAC, CE diagrams and affinity diagrams. Another is an internal customer survey.

CEDAC, CE Diagrams, Affinity Diagram

Someone with an unrefined idea can benefit from participating or creating a CEDAC or a CE diagram or affinity diagram. The idea must be put forth with a number of other ideas. CEDAC and affinity diagrams were described in previous sections. Sharing the ideas and taking part in the process of grouping the ideas often leads the idea generator to see a slightly different angle that could improve their idea. They may also see how their idea could be combined with another idea to create a new idea.

Internal Customer Survey

An internal customer survey can also help refine an idea by giving the idea generator feedback. The internal customers to be surveyed should be those individuals who will feel the effects of the idea and anyone else that might offer good input.

The survey should give a brief description of the idea and, in bullet form, its features and benefits. A feature is what it will do and a benefit is why doing that is good for the process or the people. For example, an air bag is a feature of a car. Its benefit is that it can prevent the driver from hitting the steering wheel in a front-end collision. In the survey, each feature should be described in detail so that the person surveyed has enough information to be able to offer improvement suggestions.

The internal customer survey will have a question for each feature/benefit to get feedback on the value of an idea, plus several questions about how to improve the idea. The types of questions can be true-false, yes or no, multiple choice, and open-ended, among others. One approach to surveying an improvement idea is to use a combination of multiple choice, yes or no, and open-ended. Table 7.4 shows an example.

TABLE 7.4.   Internal Customer Survey (partial)

Question 10

Replacing the four bolts with two quick-action clamps will reduce the product changeover time by 12 minutes and eliminate the chance we'll hit our hands on the sides of the unit. How important is this feature and its benefits to you?

A. Crucial—the quick-change clamps must be installed to eliminate the chance of an accident occurring.

B. Very important—the clamps are very important to improve safety and my job overall.

C. Somewhat important—the clamps will improve safety a little but not significantly.

D. Not important at all—the clamps would not improve my job nor improve safety.

Question 11

Do you have any ideas to improve the clamping?   Yes/No

Question 12

If you answered yes to question 11, how would you improve it?

Tools for Presenting Ideas for Approval

Ideas that are beyond the supervisor's boundaries of freedom must be approved by the EDIS steering committee or by top management. In many cases, the idea generator must "sell" the idea to one of these groups. Some of the simple tools of continuous improvement can be used by the idea generators to help sell their ideas. Data-presentation tools can be used to show the current state as well as to display projections of the improvements made by implementing the idea. Other tools can be used to show how the process currently flows and how the idea will improve the process flow.

Data-Presentation Techniques

The same techniques described earlier as tools for identifying areas needing improvement ideas can be used to sell an idea to the EDIS steering committee or to top management. A histogram can show outliers from the normal process variation to support the need for an improvement idea. An improvement idea can be supported with a concentration diagram that shows where a problem is located. Bar graphs, line graphs, pie charts, scatter diagrams, and trend charts put data into different pictures that can help prove the need for an improvement idea. A tally sheet (Figure 7.24) can describe where a problem lies to assist the approval process.

All of these data presentation techniques cannot only show the current state of the process, they can also describe the improvements projected as a result of implementing an idea. This comparison of the current state versus the improved state can often sway the approval body to approve the idea.

Showing the Process Flow

Flowcharts, brown-paper flowcharts, and workflow diagrams were all described earlier in this chapter. Besides being tools to help generate ideas, they can also be invaluable to idea generators to help them prove the necessity of their ideas. These tools can visually show the inefficiencies or problems in the process that the idea will improve.

Cause of Rejection	Number Made = _212_	Total Rejections By Cause
• Scratched Door	|||	3
• Missing Hardware	⊥⊦⊦⊤ |||	8
• Broken Glass	|	1
• Door Won't Fit	⊥⊦⊦⊤	5
• Scratched Top	||	2
• Scratched Right Side	|	1
• Scratched Left Side		0
• Other	||	2
	Total Rejections	22

FIGURE 7.24. Tally Sheet

Showing the process flow as it is now and as it is projected to improve can be a dramatic way to get an idea approved.

Tools for Implementing Ideas

Once an idea is approved, it must be put into place. This is usually the most inefficient part of the EDIS. One reason for this is that implementation is the hardest part. However, it's only the hardest part because historically we haven't given our employees the proper tools to implement improvements. Tools such as checklists, Program Evaluation and Review Technique (PERT) charts, and activity plans will help the generator to implement their improvement idea with minimal problems and in a time-efficient manner.

Checklist

A checklist keeps track of items or activities. In implementing an improvement idea, a checklist keeps track of the items and activities needed to complete the idea. Checklists can be created by each idea generator for the specific items or activities needed for a specific idea. A better approach is to have a generic checklist for companywide use

Idea Number: _____   Date:_____
Originator: _____

☐ 1. Idea reviewed with other shifts

☐ 2. Idea reviewed with all affected departments

☐ 3. List items needing to be purchased. Check first box
     when requisitioned and second when received

        ☐ ☐ _____

        ☐ ☐ _____

        ☐ ☐ _____

        ☐ ☐ _____

☐ 4. Work order written

☐ 5. Procedures revised

☐ 6. Others
       ☐ _____

       ☐ _____

       ☐ _____

FIGURE 7.25.   EDIS Ideas Implementation Checklist

that each idea generator could customize to his or her idea. An example of a checklist is shown is Figure 7.25.

PERT Chart

Implementing an idea doesn't always just follow along in a series from one activity to the next. In order to implement an idea most efficiently, we usually have to engage in several activities simultaneously. It's tough to keep everything straight when we have to do several things at once. We often overlook things or don't work on the most important ones at the right time so the implementation drags on. We can avoid most of these problems using a PERT chart. A PERT chart helps us identify the parallel activities (paths) that we must complete in order to implement the idea. It will help us focus on the critical path. This is the group of activities that takes the longest to complete. We can't complete the implementation in less time than the critical path, but if activities on the critical path go beyond the time estimated, the whole idea implementation process will grow longer.

The U.S. Navy developed PERT in the late 1950s as a way to coordinate the work of the many subcontractors working on the Polaris Missile Program. The Navy estimates the use of PERT reduced the Polaris project by two years. Now many people use PERT to plan, control, and monitor the progress of large projects. We do not recommend using PERT in its official or classic form. We recommend an adaptation of PERT that we'll call Simple PERT as a way to implement ideas.

The steps to constructing a PERT chart are:

1. Clearly define the specific objective of your PERT chart.
2. Determine and list the individual activities (or steps) that will be needed to implement your idea. This is a good time to brainstorm. Don't worry if you can't think of every activity now; you can add more activities later, if necessary.
3. Build a table called an activity list with four columns like this:

Activity Letter	Activity Step	Immediate Predecessor	Time For Activity
A	Start	—	—
.	.	.	.
.	.	.	.
.	.	.	.

4. Write the activities in column 2. It helps to put activities in the order in which they should be completed, as best you can. Assign a corresponding activity letter (A, B, C, and so on) in column 1. Always begin with "Start" (activity A) and finish with "Complete" or "End."

TABLE 7.5.   Simple PERT Activity List

Objective: Install a single service line

Activity Letter	Activity Step	Immediate Predecessor	Time (Days) For Activity
A	Start	NONE	—
B	Determine railing layout	A	2
C	Get quotes on railings	B	5
D	Choose railing style	C	1
E	Order railing (including delivery lead time)	D	15
F	Move furnishings	E	1/2
G	Install railing	F	1/2
H	Design sign	A	1
I	Get quotes for sign	H	7
J	Order sign (including delivery lead time)	I	20
K	Install sign	J	1/2
L	Write/send letter to surveyed customers	A	5
M	Design PR poster	A	2
N	Mount PR poster	M	1/2
O	End	G+K+L+N	—

5. Determine which activities must immediately precede each activity on the list. Look at each activity and ask what must be completed before we can do this activity. Write the appropriate activity letters in column 3. (Often, it is at this point that the required activities we forgot will become obvious. Keep expanding the list but don't add any trivial items.)

6. How long will it take to do each activity? Write the time in column 4. Usually the time estimate will be in term of days, but sometimes we may use hours or weeks depending on the project. Table 7.5 shows an activity list for implementing an idea for a single line at a bank to improve customer satisfaction with teller transactions.

7. Construct the PERT chart.

   a. Draw a circle on the righthand side of a sheet of paper. This represents the end result or the completed project.

   b. Draw arrows pointing to the circle for each activity that is an immediate predecessor of the "project completion." Label each arrow with its activity letter.

   c. Now draw a circle at the beginning of each arrow. (See Figure 7.26 for an example.)

   d. Back up farther on the chart and now draw the arrow for activities that are the immediate predecessors for the circles just drawn. Remember to label the arrows with the appropriate activity letter.

   e. Continue until all of the activities are on the PERT diagram.

   f. The diagram should always begin and end with a single circle.

   g. Be sure each arrow is labeled.

   h. Write the time values for each activity onto the PERT chart.

   Figure 7.27 shows Step A through the final step for the bank single-service line.

8. A Simple PERT chart will have one or more activity paths (routes) from the start of the project to the finish. Now find the time for each activity path by adding all the time values for activities in that path from start to end. Using Figure 7.27 as an example, the activity path lengths are shown on Table 7.6.

   Surprisingly, the longest activity path in Table 7.6 isn't the one with the most steps. Activity path A-H-I-J-K-O, the series of steps

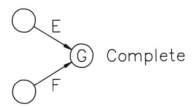

FIGURE 7.26.   Starting a PERT Chart at the End

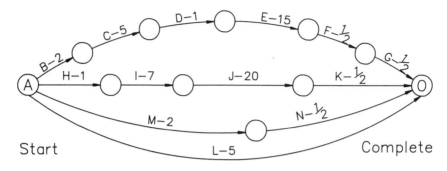

FIGURE 7.27. Completed PERT Chart

involved in the sign purchase and installation, is the longest path at 28½ days. This is the critical path. The quickest the project can be completed is the time it takes to complete the longest path. Things can happen to make the project longer, but not shorter unless we provide more resources. We always need to stay on top of activities on the critical path because it controls the time of the entire idea implementation. If activity path A-H-I-J-K-O takes longer than 28½ days, then the idea implementation takes longer.

A PERT chart often is used hand-in-hand with an activity plan, which is described next.

Activity Plan

Activity plans are a logical extension of PERT charts. Like a "what, who, when," action plan for a simple project, the activity plan spells out the details on how the necessary activities will be completed.

TABLE 7.6. Calculating the Activity-Path Length

Activity Path	Time for Each Activity	Total Time
A-B-C-D-E-F-G-O	2+5+1+15+ ½+ ½	24 days
A-H-I-J-K-O	1+7+20+ ½	28½ days
A-M-N-O	2+ ½	2½ days
A-L-O	5	5 days

ACTIVITY PLAN FOR: _____

ACTIVITY PATH	ACTIVITY	WHO	TIME SCALE (EG: MIN., HOURS, OR DAYS)
I (THE LONGEST PATH)			
II			
III			
IV			
o			
o			
o			

FIGURE 7.28. Activity Plan Format

Activity plans can be developed without PERT charts, but using a PERT chart makes sure we keep track of how the activities in the plan depend on one another.

The basic design of an activity plan is shown in Figure 7.28. We'll show how it works using the bank example described earlier under PERT charts:

1. Name the activity paths. Call the path that will take the longest time to complete Activity Path I. The next longest would be Activity Path II, and so on.

2. Do not repeat any individual activity that is already shown in a prior activity path. In our "single bank line" example, the longest path (Activity Path I) is A-H-I-J-K-O. The second longest path is A-B-C-D-E-F-G-O. Activities A and O are in both these paths. List A and O activities only in Activity Path I. Activity Path II will be B-C-D-E-F-G.

3. Use a circle to indicate the start of an activity and a triangle to show the planned completion. Put the activity letter beside the circle. As the project evolves, the circles and triangles can be shaded as an activity is started or completed; this helps track progress.

4. Within any activity path, we cannot start an activity until we have completed the one before it.

5. Often, there is a time within an activity path that requires no work from anyone. For instance, in our bank example, after ordering the sign we had a 20-day lead time before delivery. No additional work could be done by the team on that activity path until the sign was received. We call waiting periods of this type "slack time." Slack time will be indicated by a dotted line on the activity plan.

6. When we have slack time, we shouldn't stop work on the project. Use slack time to move down to the next activity path and start work there.

7. Whenever an activity step is complete, always check the status of the activity paths that are longer than the one you are working on. Remember, we must always keep the longest path moving to get the project done in the shortest possible time.

The activity plan for the bank idea is shown in Figure 7.29. Note that they had more than one person implementing the idea. This

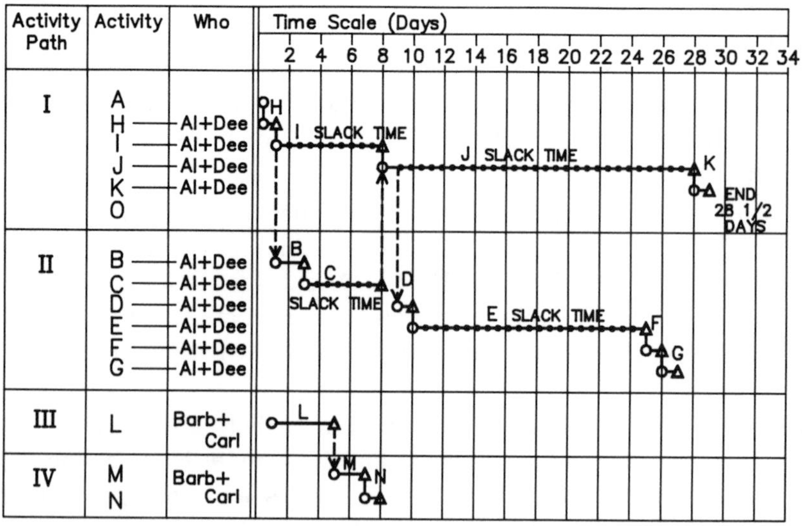

FIGURE 7.29.   Completed Activity Plan

demonstrates another advantage of creating an activity plan—it can show us (and the EDIS steering committee or top management) when we need additional help to get an idea implemented in the least amount of time.

Conclusion

This chapter has covered many of the CI tools needed as part of an EDIS. These aren't all the tools there are nor all the tools everyone will ever need in working with improvement ideas. These tools are a good basic toolbox. We all should refer to Table 7.1 often to remind ourselves of the tools we have for now. Later, we'll need more advanced CI tools, but don't forget these basic ones. Those we have here will help us make many improvements.

Chapter 8

Success Stories:
Stealing Shamelessly

Up to this point we've introduced the concepts behind an Employee-Driven Idea System (EDIS) and described the process for setting one up. In this chapter, we will review the idea systems of eight organizations. Each of these idea systems differs slightly from the rest—each has adapted an EDIS to their environment. The eight organizations range from small to large companies in both the manufacturing and service sectors, showing that an EDIS can work for all. The eight also differ in the state of evolution in their idea system, starting with Sheldahl, Inc., which has had an EDIS in place for several years and serves as a benchmark organization in this area, to Turbotec Products, Inc., which just recently introduced an EDIS. The eight organizations described in this chapter are:

- Sheldahl, Inc.
- A Connecticut-based truck-component manufacturer[1]
- Honda of America Manufacturing

---

[1]This company's policy is to remain anonymous in published materials although it is willing to share information.

- Rockwell Space Operations Company
- Critikon, Inc.
- AT&T Universal Card Services
- Toyota Motor Manufacturing, U.S.A., Inc.
- Turbotec Products, Inc.

Despite the differences among these organizations' idea systems, it is important to note that the EDIS of all eight of them have some similarities. It is the following similarities that have made these idea systems successful:

- All strive for rapid approval and implementation of ideas.
- All involve the idea maker in the implementation (some involve the idea maker but do not allow them to implement the idea if the scope of it is beyond his or her ability).
- All rely on the role of the supervisors as idea coaches as the key to their system.
- All recognize the idea makers for their ideas.
- All put their employees through an overview of the EDIS, train them in how the system works, and conduct training in continuous improvement (CI) tools.
- All incorporate their idea system as an integral part of their overall total quality (TQ) efforts.

Sheldahl, Inc.

In early 1987, Sheldahl, Inc., a Minnesota-based manufacturer of electronic interconnects, started an EDIS. Since that time Sheldahl's Implemented Suggestion System (ISS) has evolved into a model system for involving production employees in creating and implementing their own ideas. In February 1993, Judy Stadler, employee relations manager and ISS administrator, shared a speaking platform on suggestion systems with Toyota and Honda, two organizations noted for their idea systems.

Sheldahl spent a significant amount of time designing ISS before its introduction. This effort resulted in the ISS manual,[2] which served to document the system as well as provide the basis for employee training on how the system works. This 84-page manual outlined:

- the purpose of ISS;
- the ISS kickoff, including training requirements and initial meetings;
- the mechanics of ISS;
- its administration;
- ISS recognition strategies.

Sheldahl eventually pared the ISS manual down to a 17-page working document to facilitate ease of use among employees, who were all given copies. This document covers the purpose, mechanics, and the recognition strategies of ISS.

Sheldahl's ISS is part of its CI process known as PACE (Persistent Advancement to Competitive Excellence). Each production department is measured on its level of involvement in ISS as part of the company's PACE objectives. Employees are encouraged to participate in ISS through Sheldahl's ISS recognition strategies, its visibility strategies, and by the department supervisors in their monthly meetings.

To participate in ISS, an employee with an improvement idea uses the top half of Sheldahl's implemented suggestion form (Figure 8.1) to:

- describe the idea and how it can be implemented;
- estimate costs;
- describe its benefits.

The employee reviews the idea with the supervisor, who is authorized to approve most ideas. (ISS ideas are subject to Sheldahl's regular approval policies but the cost and resource utilization for most ideas fit within the supervisor's boundaries of freedom.) Once the

---

[2]©1987, Sheldahl, Inc., Northfield, MN.

IMPLEMENTED SUGGESTION FORM

STEP I: Explain your idea as thoroughly and clearly as possible. Show how your idea will be implemented. Include cost and benefit, if possible.

Suggestion No. _____

Safety Improvement

☐ Check here.

Authorization to proceed   _____   Date _____

(Check box that applies.)

☐ Team Improvement $2.00 Cash

STEP II: Date of completion   _____   ☐ Individual Improvement $1.00 Cash
plus $1.00 credit in gift savings acct.

STEP III: Did the improvement achieve the desired results? Explain.

$2.00 ☐ Team

$1.00 ☐ Individual

Supvr. approval after comp. _____

Salaried Support Person who helped significantly on this suggestion. _____

Approved by _____

Suggestor's Name _____

Received by _____

Employee Number _____

Date_____

Acct. # 04-0077-9202

Form 5535E

FIGURE 8.1.   Sheldahl's Implemented Suggestion Form

(Reprinted with permission.)

idea is approved, the employee, with the help of the supervisor, implements the idea. The ISS Manual describes how employees can get support from their supervisor and other functions to implement their idea. Once the idea is implemented, the idea maker completes the bottom of the implemented suggestion form.

A widespread recognition strategy is part of ISS as well as a way to promote it. An implemented idea earns the idea generator $1 plus $1 in gift credits that can be accumulated and redeemed at two local stores. Team ideas earn $2 cash for the team and/or $1 or $2 in gift credits per team member.

There is also monthly recognition in each department for the ideas rated best by their peers. All employees in the department rate each idea from 1 (lowest) to 10 (highest). Each department earns an award kitty of $50 to $445 based on the number of people in the department and the department's percent participation in ISS for that month. Those ideas recognized by their peers as the best earn the idea maker part of the kitty. The number of awards in each department and the value of the award are also figured from the department's size and participation rate. There are also quarterly-awards. Each quarter, employees vote on the best ideas for the past three months. The idea receiving the most points earns $100 for the idea maker. The quarterly winners from each department are further recognized at an annual luncheon hosted by Sheldahl's management team.

A random drawing is held each month for all implemented ideas. The winner receives a day off with pay and a member of the management team fills in for that employee.

The most valuable implemented idea from a safety standpoint is chosen monthly by the companywide safety committee. That idea maker also receives a day off with pay and further recognition at the annual luncheon.

The nonreward recognition approach plays an even more important role in the success of ISS. Each month, pictures of those with the winning ideas are posted in trophy cases. To recognize departmental participation, each month a "traveling" trophy is presented to the department with the greatest participation in ISS. The trophy is presented at a special break, and refreshments are served to the entire department.

Idea makers are also given the opportunity to recognize the people who helped them with their idea. At the bottom of the implemented suggestion form, there is a space for the idea maker to recognize the "salaried support person who helped significantly on this suggestion." Each month, everyone recognized by the idea makers for their support are included in a random drawing. The winner receives further recognition.

Judy Stadler reports that work has constantly gone into improving Sheldahl's Implemented Suggestion System. Judy leads an annual ad hoc team (from all levels in the organization) that reviews the system and sets plans for improvements. In the near term, their improvement efforts will focus on establishing a follow-up system to determine the status of an improvement after six months.

Sheldahl's efforts have paid off. Participation in ISS has averaged over two ideas per employee per year for the last two years, an improvement of over 35 percent from the previous two-year period. ISS remains a key component of the PACE to keep Sheldahl a leader in the highly competitive electronic interconnects marketplace.

Truck Component Manufacturing Company

Few American companies have penetrated the supply lines for components to vehicle manufacturers in Japan. The organization whose idea system we'll describe in this section is one of the few that has. This manufacturer of truck braking systems feels it owes its success in penetrating the Japanese market to their *Kaizen* CI Process. One of the critical parts of its *Kaizen* activities is its EDIS. In 1992, this idea system generated an average of 4.2 improvement ideas per eligible employee. The idea approval and implementation rates were at 100 percent. (This company is a unionized facility; currently, EDIS participation is limited to bargaining-unit and nonexempt hourly employees.) The ideas from the EDIS had a positive impact on many of its performance indicators, including productivity, safety, quality, and customer satisfaction.

Their EDIS was established in 1989. It is administered by a team of three. This team tracks the status of ideas, measures the EDIS performance against its goals for participation and ideas per employee, and audits the process.

The key to the EDIS is not the administrative team. It has always been the idea coaches (or the supervisors) who have driven the process to success. The supervisors help the employees fill out the idea forms (Figure 8.2), approve the ideas, and help the employees implement the ideas. Each idea generator can draw up to $50 from petty cash to implement the idea. Ideas costing more must go through the purchase-order process. Once an idea is implemented, the supervisor signs off on the implementation and the idea is entered into the idea reward/recognition system.

Each implemented idea earns a $4 award certificate for an individual and a $2 award certificate for each team member for a group idea. This manufacturer is organized into cells targeted at specific customers. Each month, the cell operations managers select the top ideas from their cells (each can select up to three depending on their cell's participation rate) and submit them to a panel of judges. These judges are drawn from the pool of employees who have won a monthly award previously. This creates a pool of peers that select the top three ideas for the month. There are awards for the top three ideas each month:

- *First Place.* $35 award certificate, a framed certificate, and the choice of three shares of stock or a clothing item embroidered with the company logo.

- *Second Place.* $25 award certificate, a framed certificate, and the choice of two shares of stock or a clothing item embroidered with the company logo.

- *Third Place.* $20 award certificate, a framed certificate, and the choice of one share of stock or a clothing item embroidered with the company logo.

From the 12 monthly first-place ideas, the best idea of the year is chosen by the president's staff with an award of $250 going to the generator of the winning idea. The award certificates are redeemable at any time for gift certificates to local stores (choice of two stores) or for stock (at its value on the first of the current month).

CONTINUOUS IMPROVEMENT FORM

Suggestor's Name(s) _____

IS Team Name _____ Dept No. _____ Shift _____

My Improvement Idea is (Use additional sheet if more space is needed):

Current Method of Operation:

> PHOTO OR SKETCH

New Method of Operation:

> PHOTO OR SKETCH

Supervisor's Signature _____ Date _____ Implementation Date: _____
(Check benefits on reverse side)

FIGURE 8.2.   Truck Component Manufacturer's Idea Form

(Reprinted with permission.)

Benefits of Operation Improvement (Check all applicable):

_____ Improve Cycle Time	_____ Reduce Energy Usage	_____ Improve Delivery
_____ Increase Tooling Life	_____ Decrease Handling	_____ Improve Quality
_____ Reduce Inventory	_____ Improve Safety	_____ Reduce Downtime
_____ Improve Process	_____ Improve Cust. Satisfaction	_____ Decrease Scrap/Rework
_____ Improve Morale	_____ Improve 5S's	_____ Improve Productivity
_____ Reduce Error (Poke Yoke)	_____ Improve SMED	_____ Improve Visual Control
_____ Other (Explain)		

WHY?

(((1)))

Problem: _____
_____
_____

WHY?

(((2)))

Cause: _____
_____
_____

WHY?

(((3)))

Cause: _____
_____
_____

WHY?

(((4)))

Cause: _____
_____
_____

WHY?

(((5)))

Root
Cause: _____
_____
_____

In their EDIS, there is also one more award, the day-off-with-pay award. This is awarded based on a random drawing each month from all of the suggestions implemented in that month.

All awards are presented by upper management in the cell or department where the award winner works. In addition, the EDIS is always on the agenda for the companywide monthly communication's meeting.

Pictures are a large part of the recognition strategy. Pictures of the award winners are posted prominently at the facility entrance. The company newspaper covers winning ideas each issue. There is also recognition for the cell or department that has the highest EDIS participation rate for the month. This group receives a display ribbon along with coffee and donuts.

As part of its *kaizen* activities, the employees are constantly striving to improve everything they do. The EDIS is no exception. They are constantly working to improve it, to make it more effective. The changes have been small but steady, just like a solid *kaizen* process. The major change since the program's inception has been to change the monthly award-selection process; they are now chosen by a committee of peers. Winning ideas are chosen by a committee of the previous award winners. The idea-system administrator believes this change was the catalyst that increased the EDIS participation rate from averaging just over one idea per employee to the 4.2 ideas per employee average reached in 1992. This company expects that its EDIS will remain a critical component of *Kaizen* and will help them continue to supply to U.S. and Japanese truck manufacturers, as well as penetrate the European market.

Honda of America Manufacturing

Honda of America Manufacturing has one of the best known and most successful EDIS's in this country. Pat Stidham of Honda of America's Maryville, Ohio, staff oversees the Honda of America Suggestion System. She reports:

> "We realize our key asset is the associate. We rely on them to bring new, fresh ideas into their processes. Empowering the associates

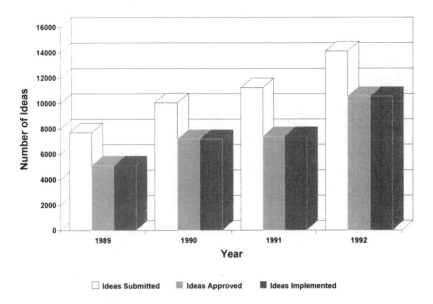

FIGURE 8.3. Suggestion System Results

reaps large benefits for the corporation and builds self-esteem. It provides them with the opportunity to make a difference in *their* company."[3]

The results speak for themselves as shown in Figures 8.3 and 8.4. While the number of eligible employees from 1989 to 1992 remained roughly the same, the number of ideas, number of approved and implemented ideas, and the percentage of eligible employees participating have increased each year.

All hourly associates at Honda of America are eligible to participate in the suggestion system. An associate with an improvement idea fills out a suggestion form and submits it to his or her department. Each department at Honda of America decides on the approval authority for ideas. Most ideas can be approved by the supervisor and can be implemented directly by the associate with support from the supervisor. Ideas that are larger in scope are submitted for ap-

---

[3]Personal communication.

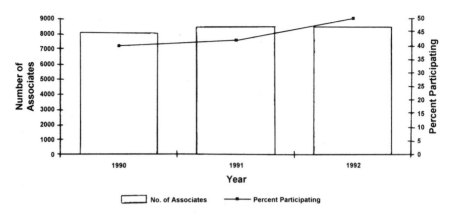

FIGURE 8.4.   Associate Participation Rate

proval and involve the department manager. Departments have suggestion system facilitators who monitor the process and ensure that the associates receive a feedback form on their idea within seven days. For these larger-scope ideas, the associate will be involved in the implementation but may or may not be the idea implementer.

The Honda of America Suggestion System is part of Honda of America's Voluntary Involvement Program (VIP). When the associate has the idea fully implemented, he or she receives VIP points and a small monetary award. (VIP points accumulate over an associate's career and special awards are given at selected milestones.) In addition, the associate is recognized for the idea in front of department peers by the department manager. Outstanding ideas are recognized in front of the entire plant including the plant manager and the president of Honda of America.

Honda of America participates in the National Suggestion Contest held annually by the Employee Involvement Association (formerly the National Association of Suggestion Systems). Honda of America associates have received national recognition for placing high in this contest.

Honda of America Manufacturing has made no major changes in its suggestion system over the last three years. This lack of recent major changes reflects the efforts to refine the idea system right after it was kicked off in 1985. Among these early refinements was simplifying the process to allow ideas to speed through. This created a solid idea system that Honda of America has worked to make small, steady improvements to. One recent improvement it reported was the updating of their idea system data base onto its mainframe computer system. This constant improvement has created one of the most recognized idea systems in America; a refined EDIS that has become a catalyst for improving all processes at Honda of America.

Rockwell Space Operations Company

In the 1960s, the space community was the worldwide leader in continuous improvement and innovation as NASA, and its suppliers stretched to reach the vision set forth for them by President Kennedy: "To land a man on the moon before this decade is out and return him safely to earth."[4]

Rockwell Space Operations Company (RSOC), a subsidiary of Rockwell International Corporation, has worked to continue this legacy of continuous improvement with its Operations Excellence TQ effort. One of its sources of direction for improvement has become its employee-idea system.

RSOC's employee-idea system evolved differently than many other successful EDIS's. In most large organizations, an EDIS is designed for the whole organization, piloted in selected areas, modified where needed, and then rolled out to the rest of the organization. RSOC's idea system has its roots as an intrapreneurial effort of one group within RSOC to generate improvement ideas in an environment in which a traditional suggestion system was not working. (It was slow, bureaucratic, and included too many constraints.)

RSOC had previously used a traditional, centralized suggestion system. This program was reward-based; the suggestors could earn up to 10 percent of the cost savings from their suggestions. It restricted the submission of ideas to only those "out of job" scope. The Flight Design & Dynamics Operations group at RSOC recognized that the traditional suggestion system was not working. Flight Design was averaging 0.23 suggestions per person per year with only 37.5 percent of those suggestions adopted. They knew that something

---

[4]This quote appears on a plaque at the Kennedy Space Center in Cape Canaveral, FL.

had to be done to tap the improvement ideas of its employees. The Flight Design Employee Idea Program (EIP) was the result of a Flight Design improvement team effort to get at the root cause of the problem, to identify a solution, and to put the solution in place.

Flight Design's EIP involved all employees at all levels in the operation and encompassed ideas both within and outside the employee's job scope. It even involved employees from their customer, NASA, and from RSOC subcontractors. Ideas submitted were evaluated by the idea maker's supervisor. In many cases, the supervisor authorized the idea. Depending on the scope, however, approval would be made at the level designated by RSOC policies. Once approved, the idea maker implemented the idea or was involved in the implementation.

EIP in Flight Design promoted immediate recognition over monetary rewards. Idea makers were given immediate recognition from their supervisors and recognition awards were presented to individuals and groups based on their involvement in EIP.

As a result of EIP, the rate of ideas submitted climbed tenfold in Flight Design. Implemented ideas have improved everything from daily work practices to mission engineering policies.

At its start, Flight Design's EIP was integrated with the corporate employee suggestion program. Some of the initial ideas submitted into EIP were later transferred into the traditional suggestion program. This was discontinued when the company dismantled the traditional employee suggestion program. With the discontinuation of the traditional companywide suggestion program, the Flight Design EIP stood out even more. Recognizing its success, RSOC management opted to use the intrapreneurial EIP effort as a model for a new RSOC companywide EDIS. In reviewing the Flight Design's EIP, some important points were learned:

- Several Flight Design groups had much higher participation rates than their counterparts;
- Employees in the groups with higher participation rates were better informed of the EIP;
- These high-participation groups had stronger CI efforts than other groups.

RSOC used this information to design its companywide idea system that will be rolled out this year. The idea system, renamed ACTS (Achieving Continuous Team Success) was designed by a team led by Deed Vest, director of organization development and Joel Lowe, systems engineer, and included membership from their customer and the other subcontractors. The team modified some features of Flight Design's EIP:

- Ideas are approved by local (department) committees
- When an idea is implemented, the tangible benefits are captured as part of the justification for a company gain-sharing program
- Documentation is based on a model that closely parallels that used by the customer, NASA. This greatly reduced duplication and confusion.
- Implemented ideas are still recognized in the local work groups. In addition, ideas resulting in major improvements are recognized companywide.

Taking the idea system companywide coupled with the involvement of its customer and suppliers (their subcontractors) will help ensure that RSOC continues its journey of continuous improvement and satisfies its customer along the way.

Critikon, Inc.

Critikon, Inc., a Johnson & Johnson company, manufactures millions of intravenous (IV) catheters each year in its Southington, Connecticut plant. Its market is one in which even 99.9 percent quality is not good enough. A product malfunction can be extremely painful and potentially dangerous for the patient and embarrassing and costly for the health professional. Critikon's CI Process constantly pushes the organization toward zero failures. Its Ideas of Champions program aims to harness the improvement suggestions made by individuals and groups to help improve its operations, the value it provides to customers, and the performance of its products.

Ideas of Champions is open to all Critikon employees, full-time, part-time, and even contract employees. But not all ideas are eligible. Ideas of Champions does not include ideas that:

- identify a problem without offering a solution
- are not constructive (e.g., complaints)
- relate to matters already under consideration
- relate to compensation, benefits, or policies
- are actually routine maintenance items

Employees submit their ideas on an Ideas of Champions submission form (Figure 8.5). The idea maker works through the evaluation with his or her supervisor and with other affected areas. If the idea is determined to be feasible and adoptable, the idea maker will be assigned to lead the implementation where appropriate (e.g., when the scope is within his or her skill level).

At Critikon, the idea maker is recognized after an idea is implemented, not when it is submitted. The department manager recognizes the idea maker in front of his or her peers at department meetings. In addition, the supervisor awards the idea maker with one of the following small gifts:

- pins
- mouse pads
- mugs
- car washes
- lunches
- orchestra tickets

- pens
- paper-clip holders
- tanks of gas
- parking spaces
- dinners
- up to $25 cash

For ideas that increase the company's profitability by more than $20,000, the supervisors are encouraged to recognize the idea maker by submitting the idea and its results into the Johnson & Johnson Achievement Award system.

Ideas of Champions is overseen by a team of management and manufacturing associates led by Lou Pfersick, purchasing manager.

IDEA #_____

IDEAS
OF CHAMPIONS

SUBMISSION FORM

Critikon, Inc.
Champions of Innovative Products and Services Unparalleled in Customer Value

Initiator: _____   Submission Type: ☐ Individual *or* ☐ Group
Date Submitted: _____   (All member names must be listed below.)
Group Members:_____

Title: (A short description of the improvement opportunity)

|_|_|_|_|_|_|_|_|_|_|_|_|_|_|_|_|_|_|_|_|_|_|_|_|_|_|_|_|_|_|_|_|_|_|_|_|_|_|_|_|_|_|_|

Current Conditions: (Please be specific and provide as much information as possible.)

Proposed Improvement: (Attach additional supporting information, if necessary.)

Quality Fundamentals: (Please note the use of quality fundamentals in the proposed improvement.)

☐ **Customer Driven Quality** Knowing what our customers want and having the processes to meet and exceed these expectations the first time and every time.

☐ **Process Improvement** Shifting work focus from managing functions to managing processes and streamlining those that serve the customer, eliminating non value-added work, improving quality and efficiency.

☐ **Teamwork** Making things happen through a joint effort.

☐ **Cycle Time Reduction** Improving the time it takes to cycle through a process from start to finish.

☐ **Continuous Improvement** Seeking to serve our customers better, continuously surpassing their expectations and challenging ourselves to reach new levels of excellence in everything we do.

☐ **Prevention** Eliminating the potential for errors in a process.

☐ **Zero Defects** Delivering defect-free products and services to the customer (internal and external).

☐ **Supplier Involvement** Inviting our suppliers to partner with us to meet and continuously improve performance against requirements which are critical to our ability to meet and exceed our customers' expectations.

☐ **Benchmarking** Measuring Critikon's operations versus the "Best-in-Class" companies both in and outside our industry.

☐ **Management by Fact** Establishing reliable measurement systems to determine how well we are meeting our customers' expectations, measuring the effectiveness and efficiency of our processes, learning from the experiences of other companies and making operating decisions based on sound data and analysis.

Results (Please note the specific results experienced because of the improvement.)

Cycle Time Reduction: _____   Inventory Reduction:_____   Defect Reduction: _____
WIP Reduction: _____   Increased Yield: _____   Waste Reduction: _____
Space Utilization: _____   Unit Cost Reduction: _____   Other:_____

FROM: _____

TO: _____

FIGURE 8.5. Critikon's Idea Form

(Reprinted with permission.)

This team regularly reviews the idea system and its recognition strategies to ensure Ideas of Champions remains a key cog in Critikon's drive for better and more consistent processes and products.

AT&T Universal Card Services

In October 1992, AT&T Universal Card Services (UCS) won the Malcolm Baldrige National Quality Award in the Services category. Winning the Baldrige is a major achievement for any company; for one less than three years old, it is astonishing.

The key to UCS' win was the company's focus on delighting its customers; a focus that is ingrained in the UCS associates who serve those customers. This newcomer to the bankcard industry constantly seeks improvement, and seeks improvement tips from a variety of sources—including the associates themselves. The UCS "Your Ideas–Your Universe" program provides one opportunity for associates to put forth their ideas—and to see those ideas implemented.

Your Ideas–Your Universe combines a traditional suggestion program with an employee-driven idea system. This program seeks ideas from everyone in the organization, though managers are limited to suggestions outside their own departments or in areas not included in their functional expertise. In 1992 UCS' 2,500 associates averaged 4.6 ideas per person. Over 1,500 of the ideas were implemented by year end.

The mechanics of the program have been streamlined for quick action. To submit an idea, an associate fills out an idea form or calls the idea hotline and submits it to the idea program, where it is assigned to a subject-matter expert for evaluation. The subject-matter expert is not necessarily a manager. Some departments have their own associate review council who evaluates the ideas. The associate receives a silver dollar as recognition for making the suggestion.

The idea program is committed to acknowledging the suggester's idea within 24 hours and assigning the evaluator within 48 hours. These two measurements are part of their quality indicators that UCS uses.

The evaluator has two weeks to respond to the idea. The idea program sends out a reminder letter to the evaluators four days before the response is due to ensure the suggestion receives a timely answer. If the idea is approved, the associate and the evaluator work together to implement it, if possible. If the needs of the business prevent the associate from devoting the necessary time to the implementation, the evaluator may implement it alone, keeping the associate informed at each step of the process.

If the idea has wide-ranging implications, the finance department also reviews it, weighing its tangible and intangible benefits. When one of these "big" ideas is approved, it's implemented by the evaluator who, again, keeps the associate who made the suggestion informed on the progress.

When an idea is implemented, the associate who submitted it is recognized by his or her manager and receives a letter of thanks. Associates who submit winning ideas also receive tangible rewards:

• Ideas that improve workplace quality	—$10 gift certificate
• Small continuous improvement ideas	—$10 gift certificate
• Ideas that help customers	—$50 gift certificate
• Cost-saving or revenue-generating ideas	—Up to $10,000

All large cash awards are presented personally by UCS' Chief Executive Officer at companywide recognition ceremonies. Smaller winning ideas are recognized in a newsletter. The group that runs the idea program also selects an "idea of the month" to further recognize associates submitting suggestions that delight customers or result in significant tangible benefits to UCS.

Gail Forsyth, ideas program manager, leads the idea program review committee, a cross-functional team of managers and associates that administers Your Ideas–Your Universe. The review committee is charged with the responsibility to:

• Oversee all idea evaluations for consistency

• Make the final determination on the awards for accepted ideas

- Monitor the implementation process
- Ensure the impact of accepted ideas is positive for all UCS departments.

The team keeps a close watch on the program using quality indicators—including associate survey results—to keep it running smoothly and continuously improved. Each year, the program is modified based on feedback from associates and data from benchmarking studies. This continuous improvement ensures that Your Ideas–Your Universe will remain a cornerstone of UCS's drive to delight its customers and its associates.

Toyota Motor Manufacturing, U.S.A., Inc.

Few organizations can boast over 38,000 improvement ideas in one year at a 98.9 percent implementation rate with 93.2 percent of their 4,020 eligible employees participating. Yet that's what hourly and first-level salaried personnel at Toyota Motor Manufacturing, U.S.A., Inc. (TMM) did last year. Since its start in June, 1989, the TMM Suggestion System has been part of TMM's *Kaizen* Continuous Improvement activities. The role it plays can be seen by its growth (Table 8.1).

Its important role can also be seen by the level of management

TABLE 8.1.   TMM Suggestion System Results

	1989	1990	1991	1992
Ideas Submitted	1,289	7,600	20,600	38,000
Percent Approved	98%	98%	99.0%	98.9%
Percent Implemented	98%	98%	99.0%	98.9%
Number of Eligible Employees	2,900	3,084	3,450	4,020
Percent of Employees Participating	12.6%	46.5%	73.1%	93.2%

commitment. The general managers and assistant general managers from every department are on area committees that oversee the TMM Suggestion System. This visible upper-management support is one of four points that Steve Ansuini, the TMM suggestion system administrator, feels makes the system work. The other three points are:

- the suggestion system has credibility,
- TMM provides solid training in how to participate in and administer the suggestion system, and
- suggestions receive quick turnaround.

The TMM Suggestion System has *credibility* because of the extraordinary rate of implementation of ideas. Employees readily submit their improvement ideas because they know the system is geared to approve them and help them get ideas implemented. And, as with all EDIS's, the idea makers implement their own ideas in most cases. They are involved or kept informed of the implementation process in the few cases they are not the idea managers.

TMM *thoroughly trains* all employees in the TMM Suggestion System. All employees were given an overview and trained in how to use the system when it was started. New employees receive an overview and training as part of their orientation. Managers and group leaders (first-level salaried employees) receive additional training on coaching employees with ideas and on approving ideas.

TMM accomplishes *fast turnaround* of ideas by having the group leaders approve many of the ideas. TMM found a large percentage of the improvement ideas cost virtually nothing to implement. Group leaders can immediately approve these ideas. TMM has clearly defined boundaries of freedom for approving the implementation of ideas. Ideas outside the boundaries established for the group leaders are reviewed for approval at higher levels in the organization. Approvals may be made at a department-manager level or a general-manager level depending on the scope. Ideas that are very large in scope or have a large impact on the business are reviewed and approved by TMM Suggestion System Area Committees. Almost 85 percent of improvement ideas are okayed within five days. (The remainder take longer due to the need to collect more data and information.)

TMM's promotion and recognition approaches also contribute to the success of the suggestion system. TMM promotes the suggestion system widely in the organization, and has an extensive and fast-acting recognition and reward strategy. The recognition, in turn, further promotes its idea system. Group leaders are trained to recognize employees when an idea is submitted; they treat the idea maker and his or her idea as being important. Employees respond positively to this. When their idea is implemented, employees earn points that they can accumulate toward merchandise certificates.

TMM also recognizes idea makers at group meetings and in the company newsletter, *Toyota Topics*. Group leaders distribute implemented idea award (point) certificates in front of the idea maker's peers at daily meetings (TMM has two daily breaks that consist of ten minutes of free time and a five-minute group meeting). Each month in *Toyota Topics*, a section is devoted to recognizing participants in the TMM suggestion system.

Last year, 635 TMM employees contributed an average of more than two improvement ideas per month. These employees were given the TMM Star Award (a lapel pin) to recognize them for their contributions.

TMM does have one problem with the number of suggestions it receives: entering the flood of ideas into their database for tracking has become an overwhelming task. To solve this problem, TMM has designed a scannable data form (Figure 8.6). It will be introduced this year to handle the projected, continuing growth in the number of improvement suggestions.

Turbotec Products Inc.

Turbotec Products manufactures high surface area heat exchangers and tubing for medical and industrial applications. As mentioned in the introduction to this chapter, it is a small company (70 employees) that is just starting an EDIS as part of its overall TQ process. Its EDIS, known as the Turbotec Idea Program, or T I P for short, was developed by a committee comprising the CFO, the national sales manager, and a manufacturing engineer. The goal was to keep T I P simple—and it is.

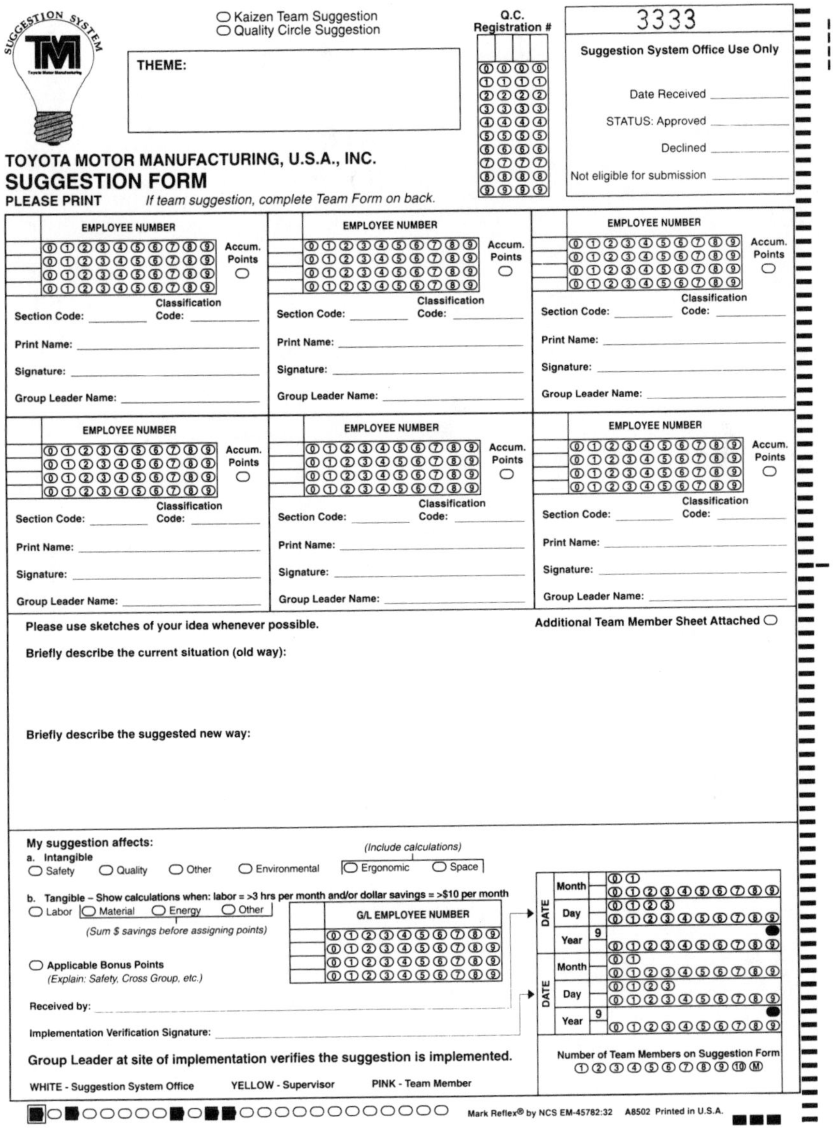
SUGGESTION SYSTEM

TMM

○ Kaizen Team Suggestion
○ Quality Circle Suggestion

THEME:

Q.C. Registration #

3333

Suggestion System Office Use Only

Date Received ______

STATUS: Approved ______

Declined ______

Not eligible for submission ______

TOYOTA MOTOR MANUFACTURING, U.S.A., INC.

SUGGESTION FORM

PLEASE PRINT *If team suggestion, complete Team Form on back.*

EMPLOYEE NUMBER — Accum. Points ○

Section Code: ______ Classification Code: ______

Print Name: ______

Signature: ______

Group Leader Name: ______

Please use sketches of your idea whenever possible.

Additional Team Member Sheet Attached ○

Briefly describe the current situation (old way):

Briefly describe the suggested new way:

My suggestion affects:

a. Intangible

○ Safety ○ Quality ○ Other ○ Environmental ○ Ergonomic ○ Space *(Include calculations)*

b. Tangible – Show calculations when: labor = >3 hrs per month and/or dollar savings = >$10 per month

○ Labor ○ Material ○ Energy ○ Other

(Sum $ savings before assigning points)

G/L EMPLOYEE NUMBER

○ Applicable Bonus Points
(Explain: Safety, Cross Group, etc.)

Received by: ______

Implementation Verification Signature: ______

DATE — Month / Day / Year 9

Group Leader at site of implementation verifies the suggestion is implemented.

Number of Team Members on Suggestion Form

WHITE - Suggestion System Office YELLOW - Supervisor PINK - Team Member

Mark Reflex® by NCS EM-45782:32 A8502 Printed in U.S.A.

FIGURE 8.6. TMM's Scannable Data Form

(Reprinted with permission.)

TURBOTEC "TIP" PROGRAM

HERE IS MY T I P

NAME(S):   DATE:
                                  FILE #:

IDEA:

Why I/we think it's a good idea:

What needs to be done to use the idea:

Supervisor's comments (including estimated cost, if known):

TIP Committee comments:

Date Reviewed with submitter(s):

Date Implemented:

FIGURE 8.7.   Turbotec Product's TIP Idea Form
(Reprinted with permission.)

Any employee can submit an idea using a T I P form (Figure 8.7) and giving it to their supervisor. The supervisor coaches them through filling it out if need be. The supervisor can approve ideas costing under $100 on the spot. Ideas costing over $100 must be approved by the supervisor and the T I P committee. Idea makers will get feedback from the T I P committee within 10 days. All ideas not approved by the supervisor receive a secondary review from the T I P committee. This is an audit tool to help the T I P committee in these early stages to assure that their supervisory training was on target.

Once an ideas is approved, the employee implements the idea with the help of the supervisor. The supervisor requisitions the money needed (up to $100) from the accounting department. Higher levels of spending go through the Turbotec Products purchasing process.

The T I P committee collects data on the ideas and files them. For each idea submitted, they recognize the idea maker with $1. For each idea implemented, the idea maker receives $5. The remainder of their recognition strategies are under development.

Because they are a small company, Turbotec Products did not pilot T I P before introducing it companywide. All supervisors and managers were introduced to T I P and trained in its procedures before it was rolled out to the organization. This was followed one week later with an introduction, training, and the kick-off to all employees. (The package of information given to employees at the introduction is included at the end of this section as Table 8.2. It shows how simple Turbotec Products has kept its EDIS.) As part of Turbotec Products' TQ implementation, all employees are being trained in CI tools using in-house resources.[5]

T I P is new at Turbotec Products, but the TQM Council and the T I P committee expect that it will rapidly become an important component in its continuous improvement drive.

---

[5]See Raymond J. Mikulak, Robin E. McDermott, and Michael R. Beauregard, *First Class Service: The Training System for Continuous Quality Improvement* (White Plains, NY: Quality Resources, 1991).

TABLE 8.2. Turbotec Products T I P Guidelines

T I P

TURBOTEC IDEA PROGRAM

Do you have any idea that would:

- Make your job better?
- Make someone else's job better?
- Improve quality?
- Reduce costs/save money?
- Make a better product?
- Change something for the better?

If so, let us hear about it—*Give us your T I P*

- Our goal is to make Turbotec the BEST!
  We need everyone's ideas.
- All ideas are good ideas.
  Small TIPs are terrific TIPs.
- Any idea submitted is rewarded with $1.00.
- Any idea implemented is rewarded with $5.00.

GOOD TIPPING!

(continued)

TABLE 8.2.   Continued

T I P
Guidelines

Q—What kind of ideas should I submit?
A—Any idea! It can be on tooling, product improvement, safety, new customers, new products, paperwork—anything, as long as it involves Turbotec.

Q—Who can submit ideas?
A—Any Turbotec employee.

Q—Can two or more employees submit the idea together?
A—Yes.

Q—When can ideas be submitted?
A—Ideas can be submitted at any time.

Q—Is there a limit to how many ideas I can submit?
A—You may submit as many as you can think of.

Q—Whom do I give my ideas to?
A—You should give them to your immediate supervisor.

Q—Do I need to write my idea on paper or can I give it verbally?
A—It is best to write it down—use the TIP forms in the cafeteria.

Q—What if I can't write it or express it too well?
A—Talk it over with your supervisor and have him/her help you fill out the form.

Q—Should I keep a copy of the idea?
A—By all means, yes.

(continued)

TABLE 8.2. Continued

Q—Will my idea earn me money?
A—Yes, you will receive $1.00 for each idea submitted and $5.00 for each idea used.

Q—What if my idea is thought of as being silly?
A—No idea will be thought of as silly.

Q—I think my idea is too small, should I still submit it?
A—Yes, you may think it's too small but small ideas are usually the best.

Q—When will I know if my idea is going to be used?
A—You will be notified no later than 10 days after you have submitted your idea. Most ideas can be evaluated immediately by your supervisor.

Q—If my supervisor thinks it's a good idea, then what happens?
A—If your idea can be put into place and costs $100 or less, then you and your supervisor can start right away. He or she has the authority to spend up to $100.

Q—If it will cost more than $100 to do, then what?
A—A TIP committee made up of your supervisor, Rocky Uccello, Bob Lieberman, and Jack Wileczka will evaluate the idea. If the idea is approved, they will authorize the necessary money.

Q—What if my supervisor does not think my idea is any good?
A—The supervisor is required to give your idea to the TIP committee for further review.

Q—When can I start submitting ideas?
A—NOW!

(*continued*)

TABLE 8.2. Continued

T I P
Supervisors' Guidelines

1. When an employee submits an idea, review it with him/her within 24 hours.
2. If you think it's a good idea, try to figure out how much it will cost to implement. Ask purchasing or manufacturing/engineering for help.
3. Initially, review all ideas with the T I P committee. Once you get the feel for it, you won't need to do this for small ideas.
4. If it will cost less than $100 to do, you and the submitter can go ahead and do it. Requisition the money you need from the accounting department, up to $100.
5. If it will cost more than $100, then you and the T I P committee will decide on a course of action.
6. Submit copies of all T I P forms to the T I P committee for filing and follow up.
7. Remember, all ideas are encouraged.
8. Maintain communication with the submitter—we want to be supportive.
9. Don't forget to submit *your* ideas!

Reprinted with permission.

Chapter 9

Epilogue: What's Next?

In Chapter 8 we looked at Employee-Driven Idea Systems (EDIS) from eight different organizations. Each differs from the others somewhat in design, but they all ring true to the EDIS philosophy. They are each at a different place in the EDIS evolution. Honda is at one end of the evolution (Stage 3, where the EDIS is making a measurable impact on the organization) relative to Turbotec, who is just beginning Stage 1. (The stages of evolution of an EDIS were described in a previous chapter.)

What happens after an organization has entered Stage 3, as Honda has? Is there a Stage 4? Has a "Stage 3" organization gone as far as they can go? Our answers are:

- No, there is not a Stage 4 for an EDIS

    but

- No, Stage 3 is not "the end," either.

The Evolution Continues

The EDIS evolution doesn't end at Stage 3. As discussed in Chapter 1, in a total quality (TQ) environment, the evolution of Employee Empowerment can be traced through four steps:

1. Continuous Improvement (CI) project teams
2. EDIS
3. Work cells
4. Self-managed work teams

These four steps are interrelated and additive in nature. The sequence lends itself to a natural evolution over time. An EDIS plays a critical role in the overall TQ Process progression. Here's why:

- To effectively work in CI project teams, employees need training in problem identification and problem-solving tools and team skills.

- CI project teams are usually crossfunctional teams working to add value and reduce waste to a process. The team scope often extends beyond the normal bounds of work of the individual team members.

- By working on a CI project team, employees can start to see a larger picture. They begin thinking in terms of internal customers and internal suppliers and of adding value to the organization as a whole, not only to their job or their department. Employees practice how to make permanent improvements by getting to the root cause within a group support structure, the CI project team. The team structure helps each team member to stay focused on the multifunctional task at hand. In short, they begin thinking *outside* of the box.

- An EDIS allows and encourages employees to use the same CI (problem-identification and problem-solving) tools on small(er) opportunities for improvement, initiating and implementing ideas themselves.

- The EDIS is a vehicle for individual expression of ideas and a source of individual recognition and a sense of worth.

- A work cell links the two; it combines the teamwork involved in a CI project team with a focus to bring *kaizen* improvements to all parts of the work cell. A work cell puts internal customers and internal suppliers together, broadening the focus of each work-cell member.

- Self-managed work teams are a natural extension of work cells.

Table 9.1 summarizes the skills gained in each step and shows how those skills help fuel the overall TQ evolution to the next step.

There is no more effective way to evolve to an effective self-managed work team approach than to use CI project team training as a foundation, add an EDIS and work through the three stages while coupling the power of the two with work cells. The evolution of the EDIS is often the missing link in the organization's move to self-managed works teams.

It is ironic that an EDIS sets the stage for self-managed work teams, but in doing so, disappears—or so it seems. In fact, an EDIS is at the genesis of a self-managed work team just as a small larva is the genesis of the Monarch butterfly. While the larva seems to disappear, it doesn't. Instead, it transforms into a majestic butterfly. An EDIS alone doesn't lead to a self-managed work team, but without the lessons of recognition, self-implementation, and communication it provides, the transformation to "the butterfly" of the self-managed work team may forever be cocooned.

The Formal EDIS Goes Informal

The EDIS is still a formal system at each of the eight organizations discussed in Chapter 8. Even Honda's version of an EDIS is formal with a "formal" administrator and a "formal" structured recognition system. However, at the Saturn Corporation (the General Motors subsidiary), the EDIS has gone informal.

According to Ron Daul, Lead Engineer at Saturn's Spring Hill, Tennessee plant:

> "We don't use a formal suggestion program. Our work teams implement their ideas as part of their jobs. Saturn's success comes from these teams and from all of our people using their skills and training to make improvements. This empowering environment is the result of our leadership team's commitment to create a dynamic, learning organization—an organization that never sleeps."[1]

---

[1] Conversation with Ron Daul, Lead Engineer of Saturn's Body Systems Panel Engineering, June, 1993.

TABLE 9.1. How Skills Gained In an Empowerment Step of a TQ Process Benefit the Next Step

TQ Employee Empowerment Step	Skills Gained in this Step	The Next TQ Empowerment Step	How the Skill Will Help in the Next Step of the TQ Process
CI Project Teams	• CI problem identification and problem-solving tools • Team skills; how to work together	EDIS	• Analyze problems and identify improvements • Working with others to implement an idea
EDIS	• Expressing and developing individual ideas for improvement • Working within the system • Recognizing others	Work Cells	• Communicating improvement ideas to other cell members • How to get things done for the cell • Respect and recognition for everyone in the cell
Work Cells	• Looking at the "big picture" • Process ownership and responsibility	Self-Managed Work Teams	• Understand that the whole organization is a series of interdependent cells or processes • Alignment; self-motivated interest in the good of the organization

Saturn has moved beyond Stage 3. Recognition is still a vital part of its work environment. Saturn knows that it is critical for team members to know that they play a vital part in the success of their team, and that their team is a vital chain in the series of linked processes that makes up Saturn. That's why Saturn placed a major emphasis on training people in recognition methods, and continues to reinforce that training.

Saturn does not have to formally administer an idea system because they feel none is needed. All team members know initiating and implementing ideas is part of their job. But Saturn created this culture from its start. Most organizations are reworking an existing culture and process. For those organizations, the formality of the EDIS is necessary, at least for the first few years. Continuing to track both the number of ideas per employee and the EDIS participation rate provides macromeasures of the health of the organization's recognition process and serves as a barometer of the health of the overall culture.

A word of caution: the move to informal status of an EDIS must be a conscious decision with planned action. Don't fool yourself by saying the EDIS is "going informal" when it is really "going down the tubes." The move to informality is a sign of a solid employee idea system that is self-sufficient, ingrained in the culture, and strong enough to live on without structure. If your system is struggling and sputtering, it is in trouble; more structure, not informality, is the prescription for a return to health.

The evolution from work cells to self-managed teams (like Saturn's) isn't easy. It should be a slow evolution, not a revolutionary leap. An EDIS, moving from stage two into stage three, will complement and improve the success of a move to self-managed work teams. Milestones of a successful evolution include:

- Expanding the boundaries of freedom
- Understanding and becoming involved in the extended process
- Increasing ownership of the process
- Providing a stake in macroimprovements, such as gainsharing

Expanding Boundaries of Freedom

The boundaries of freedom are based on the nine guideposts discussed in Chapter 1. The last four guideposts are fixed boundary stakes. The first five (monetary limits, time constraints, schedules and deadlines, access to information, and value-adding measures) are the moveable guideposts we use to structure and communicate boundaries of freedom.

Expanding boundaries of freedom involves the five moveable guideposts. Management sets the boundary limits. As the level of trust increases, the boundary limits on one or more of the five guideposts should be expanded. What drives trust? Performance drives trust; as actions of the past demonstrate trustworthiness, trust between two parties is built.

Here's an example of expanding one boundary of freedom:

- A company has begun an EDIS. The monetary limit for the implementation of any individual idea had initially been set at $50.

- The EDIS steering committee got involved in the implementation of ideas requiring more than $50. After one year of operation, the EDIS steering committee realized that it was involved in a lot of ideas. The committee members studied the pattern of the cost of idea implementation and found that 80 percent of the ideas they were involved in had a six-month or shorter payback and required $500 or less to implement.

- The steering committee presented its findings to the company's TQM Council with a recommendation to change the ceiling on spending to $500, but only for those ideas that would have a six-month (or less) financial payback. Ideas without a financial payback, or those with a payback longer than six months, still would have the $50 ceiling. The TQM Council supported the recommendation.

- The steering committee linked the guidepost dealing with monetary limits to the one regarding value-adding measures, and expanded the boundaries of freedom of the EDIS. Their next step was to communicate this new, expanded boundary of freedom to all.

Boundaries of freedom define the areas within which employees are free *to act* without additional approval. The boundaries must be clear, communicated, and consistent or else the freedoms will not be used. When boundaries of freedom are expanded, they again need to be clearly communicated and consistently applied until the boundaries are expanded again and the communication cycle starts over again.

Breaking Down External Walls

One of the most powerful extensions of boundaries of freedom involves the freedom to work with others in the organization's extended process. The extended process (depicted in Figure 9.1) is a way of looking how an organization is linked with its external suppliers and its external customers. However, in most organizations, only a few people have the right (or the freedom) to work with external suppliers and external customers and take action to improve the extended process.

In most manufacturing companies, only the sales and marketing staff routinely work with customers. The contact with suppliers may be limited to purchasing and engineering. Service organizations are different than manufacturing; usually, many people are in routine contact with customers. However, in manufacturing (where most never see the external customer) and in service organizations (where many are in steady and direct contact with customers), it is usually outside the boundaries freedom of most to act or to take the initiative to improve the extended process.

Dr. Gerald Ross and Michael Kay of Change Lab International forecast that the only successful organizations will be those in which "everyone is either serving their external customers directly, or serving someone else who is serving the customers."[2] They speak of the concept of mass customization, not mass production, where every

---

[2]From the video, *The Power of Change*, ©1992 Charthouse International, Burnsville, Minnesota.

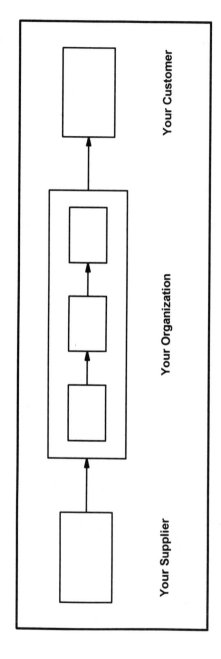

FIGURE 9.1. The Extended Process

customer and every transaction is seen as a unique opportunity to customize and to immediately, right on the spot, build additional value into the transaction for both parties.

Mass customization for the customer can only happen with mass involvement with the customer. Involvement of this type requires us to break down the walls that have historically separated one organization from the next. But, we can't remove the external walls and the safety they provide unless we replace them with boundaries of freedom. Boundaries of freedom must precede the freedom to act to meet the needs of the customized transaction.

Developing boundaries of freedom to work directly with the extended process is a development process unto itself. Employees need to learn:

- How their products and services fit into the extended process and what value they bring to this process.
- How the extended process and their role in it affects the ultimate customer.
- That they must serve the next customer in the process as well as the ultimate customer.

Each person needs understanding and insight far beyond the conventions of the past to work in the world of mass customization. The way to provide the level of understanding needed and to keep it current is to shorten the internal chain of processes that deliver products or services to the customer. Work cells do this. They shorten the chain from a long series of small, thin links to a short chain of strong, thick links. Work cells bring internal suppliers and customers together into one unified process. If the work cells are complete, each person in the cell will indeed be serving the external customer or someone else that is. And in a work cell, members become cross-skilled and gain the insight and understanding to truly serve their customers.

Rockwell Space Operations Company introduced the extended process into its EDIS: the company's external customer, NASA, and its subcontractors (suppliers) participate in the EDIS.

Allow and Encourage Process Ownership

Mass customization and work cells require a whole-person contribution to the organization. The days of checking your brains at the door and "It's not my job" must be left behind. They must be replaced with lifelong learning, training, and multi-skilling. Immediate customization can only be a reality when employees have the understanding, insight, knowledge, and skills to assimilate the information at hand, analyze it, make decisions and take action. It sounds like the work of management, doesn't it? Well, it is, but it's the work of everyone in an EDIS, and self-managed work teams take that even further.

Self-managed work teams evolve from work cells. To make the evolution, team members continue the learning process they began in the work cell, expanding their knowledge and skills beyond the conventional bounds of the job functions of the work cell. Members of self-managed work teams take ownership of many of the support functions the work cell previously relied upon. They learn and take ownership of inventory control, scheduling, budgeting, process engineering, even the hiring process. The addition of these support functions to the potential job scope of members of self-managed teams adds additional skill blocks to a skill-based pay (SBP) compensation system. Not every team member will learn every skill, but the addition of another block of skills to the capability portfolio of a team member will increase the value of that member to the organization and correspondingly increase the compensation of that member. SBP is one way of linking rewards (higher pay) and recognition of one person in a team setting.

Expanding the boundaries of freedom of a self-managed work team to include setting their own performance measures is a major step for an organization; taking this step further develops the team's sense of commitment and that goes hand-in-hand with process ownership.

It's Time to Add Rewards

Recognition is a powerful vehicle; it fuels empowerment. Early in a TQ process, rewards for specific actions provide few positives and many negatives. But when the TQ process has a solid foundation, with continuous improvement a pervasive attitude and teamwork a way of life, the time to add team-based rewards has arrived. While SBP does link rewards to the developed capability and performance of one team member, gainsharing is a parallel team-based rewards approach.

Gainsharing:

- Involves the entire team in the reward.
- Is linked directly to the performance measures for the entire team.
- Requires gains to be made before rewards can be shared.
- Gives team members a clear understanding of what they need to do to make the organization a winner.
- Assures all team members are in tune with and working toward the greater good of the organization and its customers.

When should an organization add gainsharing? We believe gainsharing is the strongest form of a team-based, performance-based reward system, but it only belongs in an organization with a solid TQ process in place. Gainsharing requires a clear long-term direction (Vision) with a commitment to ethical and moral behavior (Guiding Principles) and the tools and training to improve all processes to add value, where value is defined by the customer.

We feel the start of CI project teams is too early for gainsharing; people are just learning CI tools and how to work in a structured, focused team. The start of an EDIS is still too early. In stage one, an EDIS should focus on participation, learning implementation skills and recognition techniques. In stage two, the emphasis of the EDIS is for idea makers to improve the value-adding impact of their ideas by looking beyond the bounds of their own processes. Stage two is still too early for gainsharing.

An organization may be ready for gainsharing in stage three, when the focus of the EDIS is to increase the economic impact of the idea. If the organization has moved to work cells in the same time frame, the EDIS has begun its evolution to stage three, and gainsharing makes sense. If gainsharing is not in place as an organization evolves to self-managed work teams, we recommend adding it. Self-managed work teams can make phenomenal improvements but only if they are receiving the proper recognition and respect they deserve.

A self-managed work team without gainsharing isn't getting proper respect for the gains it generates.

Strategic Direction, Teamwork, Continuous Learning and Communication

Let's look at where we've taken the evolution of Employee Empowerment:

- We have evolved to self-managed work teams.
- SBP (skill-based pay) has arrived.
- Gainsharing is in place.
- A formal recognition system is no longer needed; recognition is built into the organization.
- Everyone is either a customer-contact person or serves someone who serves the customer.
- Self-managed work teams even establish their own performance standards.

Where does the management team fit in? Do they still have a job left to do? They sure do. Top management has the job they have always had, but rarely had time to do. Top management's jobs are to set the strategic direction, provide the resources (tools and people), establish boundaries of freedom, track the progress with macro-measures, and use data from the measures to adjust. That's what the first of the three key elements of total quality (Figure 9.2) is all about.

Creating the Environment is the job of top management; creating the environment is at the core of total quality. Top management and only top management can set the strategic direction (the Vision, Guiding Principles, and the TQM Roadmap), set the stage for the organization to be a learning organization, and establish boundaries of freedom.

The second element is the CI Toolbox. A learning organization needs everyone to speak a common language of continuous improvement and be able to use the starter kit of tools, the CI Process. The CI

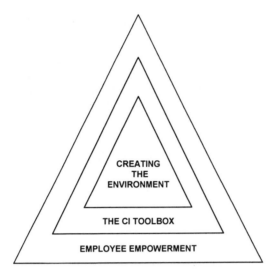

FIGURE 9.2. The Three Key Elements of TQM

Process is the catalyst for both teamwork and communication, as internal customer-supplier chains are served and barriers between processes or departments are removed. New tools are added step-wise to the starter kit as the organization becomes ready for them. A learning organization never closes the lid on its toolbox. Continuous improvement requires continuous, lifelong learning.

The third and outer element of total quality, Employee Empowerment, is derived from the first two. The evolution of empowerment includes:

- CI project teams
- EDIS
- Work cells
- Self-managed work teams

But the entire cadre of sequential empowerment options will be ineffective and self-defeating without direction, and only top management can provide that. We've come full circle.

The concepts of continuous improvement, continuous learning, and constancy of purpose are difficult to grasp and even tougher to practice. Even Saturn, with it's smooth functioning self-managed work teams is realizing how difficult it is. As noted in a recently published article about Saturn, "a surprising 29 percent [of Saturn's workforce] backed a shift toward traditional, arm's-length labor relations that would be more adversarial than the current *de facto* partnership with management."[3]

Why the seemingly high level of dissatisfaction with Saturn's innovative work teams? The article concludes it is due to the new employees brought into the workforce with a fraction of the training employees received during the start-up years at Saturn. "New employees get just 175 hours of initial schooling, compared with up to 700 hours before. And instead of first learning basic skills that are crucial to the smooth operation of Saturn's teams, such as conflict management, new hires focus on job-specific skills . . . "

It is understandable that new employees trained only in the core technologies and not in CI tools and teamwork, could be blind to the advantages a self-managed work team afforded them, not just Saturn. Without training to help them see a new paradigm, they will be blind to the responsibilities and benefits of Saturn's empowered work style.

The message here to the top management team of all organizations is that top management must lead the TQ process, not just in the beginning but forever. If top management takes a break and takes its eyes off the ball, the whole organization will strike out. Even Employee Empowerment evolved to self-managed work teams needs a strong, committed team of leaders setting the direction, reinforcing positive actions, and providing the resources needed to overcome roadblocks encountered.

What Does All This Mean?

This book isn't just about EDIS's, it's really about that third or outer element of total quality, Employee Empowerment. Employee Em-

---

[3]"Saturn: Labor's Love Lost?," *Business Week*, Feb. 8, 1993, pp. 122–123.

powerment is getting the employees to drive the quality improvement efforts of your organization, that's employee-driven quality! An EDIS is a step in that direction. It's an early step, but a large one. An EDIS can be the vehicle that helps the entire organization, individual by individual, break out of the box and work to improve the organization day in and day out.

Glossary

boundaries of freedom boundaries encompassing nine guideposts that define areas in which employees are free to act and in which they are not. Clearly spelling these out is critical to the success of an EDIS.

brainline an invisible line somewhere in the organization between the top management and the frontline employees. Those above the brainline are expected to think as part of their jobs. Those below the brainline are not expected to think, just to do. One goal in total quality is to drive the brainline out of the organization so that everyone thinks about improvements.

CI project teams groups of four to six people that are brought together to achieve a specific, focused improvement objective.

EDIS Employee-Driven Idea System; a type of suggestion system in which employees drive their own ideas for improvement through to completion.

EDIS administrator individual responsible for overseeing the administration of EDIS including logging and tracking ideas.

EDIS development team a team representing the breadth and depth of the organization with the objective of creating the EDIS.

EDIS recognition center   a bulletin board for communicating EDIS success stories and recognizing EDIS participants.

EDIS steering committee   a subcommittee of the TQM Council that oversees, audits, and directs the EDIS.

EDIS support processes   processes in purchasing, maintenance, finance, and other departments that may be needed by an idea installer to implement an improvement idea. These processes must be simplified and must be understood by all employees.

extended process   conceptually viewing your external suppliers, your organization, and your external customers as one ''extended'' process.

gainsharing   a system in which employees receive a share of the financial gains the organization has made as recognition for the role the employees have played in creating those gains.

Guiding Principles   a series of statements that defines the ethics and behaviors expected from everyone in an organization. This, combined with the Vision, give the organization direction.

idea coach   the supervisor of the idea maker. This person encourages employees to identify improvement ideas, helps idea makers to refine their ideas, and facilitates the implementation process when roadblocks appear.

idea form   a simple form to document an improvement idea and formally submit it into the EDIS.

idea initiator   the person who comes up with an improvement idea.

idea installer   the person who comes up with an improvement idea and who hopefully also is the one to implement the idea. This term also refers to individuals who help the idea generator implement an idea.

idea log   a simple data-collection form to enter ideas into EDIS. This should include space to record when an idea was submitted and when it was implemented. This does not have to be a sophisticated computerized log.

idea maker   the person who comes up with an improvement idea.

idea maker scorecard   tracks the number of ideas a person has submitted into EDIS.

idea manager   the person who comes up with an improvement idea and who hopefully will also be the one to manage its implementation. Sometimes the idea maker will need a comanager to help implement large-scope ideas.

kaizen   a Japanese term that means continuous improvement on top of continuous improvement on top of continuous improvement. It means never being satisfied with the ways things are and always looking for ways to make things better.

paradigm   the set of rules and regulations about which we view the world; the box we live in.

participation-rate thermometer   a data-display technique to show the number or percentage of employees participating in EDIS. This may be done on a department or an organizationwide basis.

peer recognition committee   a team of six to ten people established to recognize idea makers for their successes. This team should also represent the breadth and depth of the organization.

recognition   acknowledgment of contributions and accomplishments.

rewards   tangible, material or financial compensation.

self-managed work teams   teams of workers in a department or in a work cell who supervise themselves. Responsibilities associated with a traditional supervisor are rotated among team members.

skill-based pay (SBP)   a compensation system that pays people for what they know (skills), not what job function they are performing at any given time.

team ground rules   guidelines established by a team at its start-up to help ensure that it will function smoothly. These guidelines may include team logistics as well as conflict-resolution techniques that the team will adopt should a conflict arise.

TQM   total quality management. This is a culture in an organization of continuous improvement in everything, by everyone, all of the time.

TQM Council   the top management in the organization that sets the direction for the organization and leads the continuous improvement efforts.

TQM Roadmap   the strategic business plan for the organization created by the TQM Council that will guide everyone to help the organization achieve its Vision.

Vision   a short description of what the organization does and what it plans to be in the future. This is a stretch goal for the organization created by the TQM Council.

work cells   groups of internal customers and internal suppliers that are put into the same cell to work together to satisfy the needs of the external customer. Work cells are appropriate for both manufacturing and service companies.

Index